A RESEARCH GUIDE
TO SCIENCE FICTION STUDIES

GARLAND REFERENCE LIBRARY
OF THE HUMANITIES
(VOL. 87)

A RESEARCH GUIDE
TO SCIENCE FICTION STUDIES
An Annotated Checklist
of Primary and Secondary Sources
for Fantasy and Science Fiction

compiled and edited by
Marshall B. Tymn
Roger C. Schlobin
L. W. Currey

with a bibliography of doctoral dissertations
by Douglas R. Justus

GARLAND PUBLISHING, INC. • NEW YORK & LONDON
1977

Library of Congress Cataloging in Publication Data
Tymn, Marshall B   1937–
  A research guide to science fiction studies.

  (Garland reference library of the humanities; v. 87)
  Includes indexes.
  1. Reference books—Science fiction.   2. Bibliography—
Bibliography—Science fiction.   3. Science fiction—History
and criticism—Bibliography.   I. Schlobin, Roger C., joint
author.   II. Currey, L. W., joint author.   III. Title.
Z5917.S36T93   [PN3448.S45]   016.823'0876   76-52682
ISBN 0-8240-9886-2

PRINTED IN THE UNITED STATES OF AMERICA

CONTENTS

PREFACE

Academic attention to science fiction and fantasy began in 1958, when the Modern Language Association scheduled its first seminar on science fiction at its New York meeting. This seminar has met annually since then and is one of the two oldest continuing seminars of the MLA. The genre was given further impetus when the Science Fiction Research Association was established in 1970 to serve as an international clearing house for all those concerned with some phase of the study of science fiction. During the past decade, science fiction has emerged as a popular subject which has achieved critical attention and acceptance as an academic discipline. The widespread nature of this new interest in science fiction is evident in the proliferation of course offerings on the subject and in the increase in publication of works of criticism and reference to meet the demands of the scholar and teacher. Major publishers and reprint houses have supplied the need for research tools by issuing reference works and special texts in record numbers. Specialty publishers and private presses have released valuable titles that are often difficult to locate.

A Research Guide to Science Fiction Studies is designed to provide the reader—whether he be scholar, teacher, librarian, or fan—with a comprehensive listing of the important research tools that have been published in the United States and England through 1976. The volume contains over 400 selected, annotated entries covering both general and specialized sources, including general surveys, histories, genre studies, author studies, bibliographies, and indices, which span the entire range of science fiction and fantasy scholarship.

The entries are arranged into six sections: Preliminary Sources, Sources for Primary Materials, Sources for Secondary Materials, Author Studies & Bibliographies, Periodicals, and

Sources for Acquisition. Each of these sections is subdivided for access to subjects within these broad divisions. Complete alphabetical author and title indices are included to allow access to all sections. A section of doctoral dissertations is appended. This list, compiled by Douglas R. Justus, augments the sections of published works and provides a more comprehensive coverage of the genre, especially in the area of author studies and themes.

A Research Guide is intended to supplement and in some cases to supersede citations in two earlier checklists: *Science Fiction Criticism: An Annotated Checklist* by Thomas D. Clareson, and *SF Bibliographies: An Annotated Bibliography of Bibliographical Works on Science Fiction and Fantasy Fiction,* by Robert E. Briney and Edward Wood, both published in 1972. Briney and Wood and Clareson sought to compile a comprehensive listing of titles; the former supplied exhaustive coverage of bibliographical reference tools (which were, at that time, composed primarily of small editions issued by specialty publishers and fans) and the latter, while duplicating some of the bibliographical material covered in *SF Bibliographies,* concentrated on "those critical materials which are needed by the student of the genre and which have thus far made up the reaction to, and evaluation of, science fiction in the general and scholarly press" (Clareson, "Preface," p. vii). *A Research Guide* includes a number of titles listed in these pioneer checklists as well as numerous titles issued since 1972. For all selections, the editors have attempted to make critical evaluations of published material and to include only the best or most complete texts on the subject or subject author. Many of the titles in the Briney and Wood volume have been superseded by revision of existing works or by new reference tools (e.g., the 1961 edition of I. F. Clarke's *The Tale of the Future* was replaced in 1972 by a greatly enlarged second edition, while *The Robert E. Howard Fantasy Biblio,* compiled by Robert Weinberg in 1969, has been superseded by Weinberg's *The Annotated Guide to Robert E. Howard's Sword and Sorcery* and Glen Lord's definitive *The Last Celt: A Bibliography of Robert Ervin Howard,* both published in 1976). Since the numerous articles on the SF genre that have appeared in scholarly journals and popular magazines are not considered here, the researcher is referred to Clareson's *Science Fiction Criticism* and "The Year's Scholarship in Science Fiction and Fantasy" (annually in *Extrapolation*), a series compiled by Roger C. Schlobin and Marshall B. Tymn, for these items.

The editors would like to extend a note of appreciation to Douglas R. Justus for providing his exhaustive listing of dissertations and to Darlene Tymn for her assistance in preparing the indices to this volume.

Marshall B. Tymn
Roger C. Schlobin
L. W. Currey

I. PRELIMINARY SOURCES

A. GENERAL

1. Besterman, Theodore. *A World Bibliography of Bibli-ographies*. 4th ed. 5 vols. Lausanne, Switzerland: Societas Bibliographica, 1965-66.

   A list of separately published bibliographies of books and manuscripts that is international in its coverage. Entries are arranged by subject.

2. *Bibliographic Index: A Cumulative Bibliography of Bibliographies* [1937-   ]. New York: Wilson, 1938-   .

   An international list of separately published bibli-ographies and bibliographies included in books and periodicals; arranged by subject. Useful in itself and as a valuable complement to Besterman's *World Bibliography*. Issued semi-annually.

3. Mott, Frank Luther. *A History of American Magazines*. 5 vols. Cambridge, MA: Harvard University Press, 1930-68.

   A valuable reference work for its comprehensive history of the American magazine from 1741 to 1930. Contains many bibliographic references, a number of important and detailed indices, and a chronological list of magazines.

B. SCIENCE FICTION

(1) Bibliographies of Bibliographies

4. Briney, Robert E. and Edward Wood. *SF Bibliographies: An Annotated Bibliography of Bibliographical Works on Science Fiction and Fantasy Fiction*. Chicago: Advent Publishers, 1972. 49pp. [paper].

An annotated listing of approximately 100 bibliographies, indices, and checklists, many of which were published in severely limited editions now difficult to locate. Coverage is limited, for the most part, to bibliographies which were published as separate books or pamphlets, and no attempt was made to include material printed in the professional and amateur science fiction magazines. Entries are organized into four categories: magazine indices, individual author bibliographies, general indices and checklists, and foreign language bibliographies. Emphasis is on English language titles and only a small sample of foreign works is included. Access to all sections is provided through an alphabetical author/title index. Advent reports that an enlarged edition of this work is in preparation.

(2) Anonymous & Pseudonymous Literature

5. McGhan, Barry. *Science Fiction and Fantasy Pseudonyms.* rev. ed. Dearborn Heights, MI: Misfit Press, 1976. 70pp. [paper].

A revised and expanded edition of a standard work, first published in 1971, containing an alphabetical listing of the names of 945 authors and 1483 pen names.

(3) Title Changes

6. Viggiano, Michael and Donald Franson. *Science Fiction Title Changes: A Guide to the Changing Titles of Science Fiction and Fantasy Stories Published in Magazines and Books.* Seattle: The National Fantasy Fan Federation, 1965. 47pp. [paper].

An alphabetical listing by title of title changes of short stories and fictional works made up or derived from short stories published in English language books and magazines. Dated, but valuable.

(4) Classification

7. Cameron, Alastair. *Fantasy Classification System.* St. Vital, Manitoba: Canadian Science Fiction Association, 1952. 52pp. [paper].

A complex numerical system which groups the subject
matter of fantasy literature (i.e. fantasy and science
fiction) into ten major categories with scores of sub-
divisions. Each category is defined. A good beginning
for a master motif index, but the work has not been
continued. Indexed.

(5) Biography

8. Ash, Brian. *Who's Who in Science Fiction*. New York:
   Taplinger, 1976. 220pp.

   A concise collection of biographical entries for over
   400 science fiction writers, editors, artists, and
   others who have been influential in the development
   of science fiction from the era of Verne and Wells to
   the present. Each entry includes a short biography,
   and a selective bibliography. Included also are a
   brief glossary of sf terms, a partial listing of American and British sf magazines, a chronological guide
   to 100 major authors and editors, and a selective
   checklist of books on sf. Ash states that this book
   is "deliberately less than exhaustive," but numerous
   errors limit the usefulness of what could have been
   a handy one-volume reference work. Researchers are
   advised that they would be better served by Tuck's
   Encyclopedia or Reginald's *Contemporary Science Fiction Authors*, from which much of Ash's material seems
   to have been derived.

II. SOURCES FOR PRIMARY MATERIALS

A. GENERAL

9. *American Book Publishing Record* [1960-   ]. New York:
      Bowker, 1960-   .

   Contains the same information as that given in the
   weekly lists in *Publishers Weekly* except that BPR
   is arranged by subject according to Dewey Decimal
   numbers and cumulated monthly. *BPR Annual Cumulative*
   lists the monthly entries from BPR.

10. *Book Review Index* [1965-   ]. Detroit: Gale Research,
      1965-   .

   An author listing of reviews appearing in over 200
   periodicals. Covers the fields of general fiction,
   non-fiction, humanities, social sciences, librarianship and bibliography, and juvenile and young adult
   books. Issued bi-monthly with an annual cumulation.

11. *Books in Print: An Author-Title-Series Index to the
      Publishers' Trade List Annual* [1948-   ]. New York:
      Bowker, 1948-   .

   An index to the material in *Publishers' Trade List
   Annual*. Useful for finding the publisher and price
   of a book, and for finding the author's name if only
   the title is known. Issued annually.

12. British Museum. Dept. of Printed Books. *General Cata-
      logue of Printed Books*. London: Trustees, 1959-66.

   A complete record of the printed books in the Library
   of the British Museum; mainly an author catalog. Supplements issued for 1956-65 and 1966-70. The LBM is
   the most comprehensive collection of British publications in existence.

13. *Cumulative Book Index: A World List of Books in the
      English Language* [1928-   ]. New York: Wilson,
      1933-   .

Often referred to as CBI. Published periodically since 1898 with cumulations to form supplements to the *United States Catalog*. Now published monthly, except August. The *United States Catalog* and the CBI constitute a comprehensive record of American publications from 1898 to date that is indispensible for research in American literature. Each volume is a dictionary catalog with entries under author, title, and subject. Each cumulation includes a list of publishers with addresses.

14. *Library of Congress Catalog: A Cumulative List of Works Represented by Library of Congress Printed Cards, 1948-1952.* Ann Arbor: Edwards, 1953.

See description under *National Union Catalogue*. For titles issued previous to 1948 see *U.S. Library of Congress: A Catalog of Books Represented by Library of Congress Printed Cards, Issued to July 31, 1942* and its 1942-47 supplement.

15. *The National Union Catalogue: A Cumulative Author List Representing Library of Congress Printed Cards and Titles Reported by Other American Universities, 1953-1957.* Ann Arbor: Edwards, 1958.

The printed catalog of the national repository of all books and pamphlets printed in the United States. Invaluable for author citations, and for verification of bibliographic data. For titles published before 1953 see *Library of Congress Author Catalog*. Supplements cover the periods 1958-62, 1963-67, 1968-72, 1973, 1974, 1975, 1976.

16. *Paperbound Books in Print.* New York: Bowker, 1955- .

Issued in March and November of each year, each issue lists about 90,000 current paperback titles. Author, title, and subject indices.

17. *The Publishers' Trade List Annual* [1873-]. New York: Bowker, 1873- .

A bound collection of publishers' catalogs arranged alphabetically by publisher's name. Issued annually in several volumes with an index in the first volume. Information varies from complete to scant in the individual catalogs. Indexed in *Books in Print* and in the *Subject Guide to Books in Print*.

18. *Publishers Weekly*. New York: Bowker, 1872- .

Valuable as the principle vehicle for the announce-
ment of new and forthcoming books in both hardcover
and paperback format published weekly in the United
States. Occasional issues cover special topics; for
example, the science fiction issue of June 14, 1976.

19. Reginald, R. and M.R. Burgess. *Cumulative Paperback
Index, 1939-1959*. Detroit: Gale Research, 1973.

A comprehensive bibliography of approximately 14,000
mass-market paperbacks. Arranged by author and title.

20. *Subject Guide to Books in Print: An Index to the
Publishers' Trade List Annual* [1957-]. New
York: Bowker, 1957- .

A companion publication to *Books in Print*, listing
under subject the books to be found there. Issued
annually.

21. *Whitaker's Cumulative Book List*. London: Whitaker,
1924- .

A "complete list of all books published in the United
Kingdom . . . giving details as to author, title,
sub-title, size, number of pages, price, date, classification and publisher of every book." Issued
quarterly.

B. SCIENCE FICTION

(1) General Bibliographies

22. Barron, Neil, ed. *Anatomy of Wonder: Science Fiction*.
New York: Bowker, 1976. 471pp.

A yardstick for sf acquisitions for the library,
scholars, and serious fans. The bulk of this research
guide comprises two parts: the literature and the research aids. The former details over 1150 works of
fiction, organized into the following sections:
Robert Philmus on "Science Fiction: From Its Beginnings to 1870" (50 entries); Tom Clareson on "The
Emergence of the Scientific Romance, 1870-1926" (177
entries); Ivor Rogers on "The Gernsback Era, 1926-
1937" (73 entries); Joe DeBolt and John Pfeiffer on
"The Modern Period, 1938-1975" (701 entries); Francis
Molson on "Juvenile Science Fiction" (99 entries).
The latter part, compiled by Barron, lists over 125

works comprising historical and critical titles as well as bibliographies, indices, teaching aids, biographies, etc. Also listed are periodicals, literary awards, a directory of publishers, library collections, and a core collection checklist. The research aids section is by no means complete, as many of the individual lists could have been greatly expanded. Author and title index. Published simultaneously in paperback.

23. Bishop, Gerald. *New SF Published in Great Britain 1968-1969.* [Lake Jackson, TX: Joanne Burger, 1970] [paper].

The first of three volumes in this series published to date. The other volumes cover the years 1970-71 and 1972-73. The first volume contains an alphabetical listing by author only; succeeding volumes have added a title index. The 1970-71 and 1972-73 volumes also contain listings of British Science Fiction Book Club selections and non-fiction titles concerned with the sf genre. Both hardcover and paperback publications are included. Format follows that of *Whitaker's Cumulative Book List.*

24. Bleiler, Everett F. *The Checklist of Fantastic Literature: A Bibliography of Fantasy, Weird and Science Fiction Books Published in the English Language.* Chicago: Shasta, 1948. 455pp. Rpt. West Linn, OR: FAX Collector's Editions, 1972.

The pioneer fantasy checklist. Lists approximately 5300 prose titles published in the U.S. and United Kingdom from Walpole's *The Castle of Otranto* (1764) through 1947. Emphasis is on hardcover titles, but an occasional volume in paper covers is listed. The result of seven year's research, this volume remains the most comprehensive checklist in the fantasy genre.

25. Burger, Joanne. *SF Published in 1968.* Lake Jackson, TX: Joanne Burger, 1969- [paper].

An annual listing through 1976 of U.S. hardcover and paperback titles, arranged alphabetically by author and title. Commencing in 1974 the separate listings for juveniles and non-fiction were combined in the main listing.

26. Crawford, Joseph H., James J. Donahue and Donald M. Grant. *"333": A Bibliography of the Science-Fantasy Novel.* Providence, RI: The Grandon Company, 1953. 80pp. [paper].

An annotated checklist of 333 books the compilers
considered to be the best efforts in the science-
fantasy genre published through 1950. The emphasis
is on American fiction, but a few British novels are
included. Each entry classifies the work by science-
fantasy sub-genre and provides a plot summary 100 to
150 words in length. The introduction defines the
term "science-fantasy" as "an all encompassing des-
ignation of unusual fiction," and arranges this field
into eight major categories (gothic romance, weird
tale, science fiction, fantasy, lost race tale, fantastic adventure, unknown worlds, and the Oriental
tale) which are carefully defined. The entries are
arranged alphabetically by author, with a short title
index for cross reference. A useful compilation which
offers an overview of those works sought by the science-fantasy enthusiast of the 1950s.

27. Day, Bradford M. *The Checklist of Fantastic Liter-
    ature in Paperbound Books*. Denver, NY: Science-
    Fiction & Fantasy Publications, 1965. 128pp.
    [paper]. Rpt. New York: Arno Press, 1975.

Though superseded in part by R. Reginald's *Stella
Nova* and *Cumulative Paperback Index, 1939-1959,* this
index remains the only attempt at a complete survey
of fantastic literature in paperbound books and is
of great value for identifying material of the nineteenth and early twentieth centuries. This work compliments the Bleiler and Day indices of 1948 and 1963
respectively, which included few titles bound in
paper. Arranged alphabetically by author, with a
short title index for cross reference.

28. Day, Bradford M. *The Supplemental Checklist of
    Fantastic Literature*. Denver, NY: Science-Fiction
    & Fantasy Publications, 1963. 155pp. [paper]. Rpt.
    New York: Arno Press, 1975.

A listing of approximately 3000 titles which supplement those appearing in Bleiler's 1948 *Checklist* and
extends the coverage (of both American and British
imprints) through 1963. Arranged alphabetically by
author, with a short title index for cross reference.

29. Derleth, August. *Thirty Years of Arkham House 1939-
    1969*. Sauk City, WI: Arkham House, 1970. 99pp.

This volume, an enlargement of *Arkham House: The
First Twenty Years 1939-1959,* contains a brief history of the firm and a bibliography comprising a
checklist of publications through 1969 issued under
the imprints of Arkham House, Mycroft & Moran, and

Stanton & Lee. Now the best known of the specialist
fantasy publishers, Arkham House was originally founded for the express purpose of publishing the works of
H.P. Lovecraft. Derleth soon discovered a distinct,
but small, market for the fantasy and SF short story
and determined to publish collections by writers--
primarily contemporaries--other than Lovecraft. While
some science fiction was published, the emphasis was
on weird or fantasy fiction. The impact of Derleth's
publishing activities was substantial. In addition to
issuing collections by such established writers as
Algernon Blackwood, A.E. Coppard, and Lord Dunsany,
Arkham House provided a forum for new writers in the
genre, publishing many first books of fiction by now
major names in the field, including Bloch, Bradbury,
Leiber, Long, and Van Vogt.

30. Franson, Donald and Howard DeVore. *A History of the*
    Hugo, Nebula and International Fantasy Awards.
    [rev. ed.] Dearborn Heights, MI: Howard DeVore,
    1975. 104pp. [paper].

This enlarged edition of a work first published in
1971 provides information through 1975 for the Hugo
awards and through 1974 for the Nebula awards. Both
the winners and the nominees in each category are
recorded, along with notes and historical commentary.

31. Locke, George, ed. *Ferret Fantasy's Christmas Annual*
    for 1972. London: Ferret Fantasy, 1972. 76pp.
    [paper].

Pages 29-76 comprise an annotated addendum compiled
by Locke to Bleiler's 1948 *Checklist* and Day's 1963
Supplemental Checklist of approximately 300 titles,
most of which were published in Great Britain prior
to 1948. The entries are arranged alphabetically by
author with indices of illustrators and themes.

32. Locke, George, ed. *Ferret Fantasy's Christmas Annual*
    for 1973. London: Ferret Fantasy, 1974. 54pp.
    [paper].

Pages 1-27 comprise a second annotated addendum compiled by Locke to the Bleiler and Day checklists of
nearly 200 titles published prior to 1948, many of
which were published in paperback in Great Britain
during World War II. Arranged alphabetically by
author with indices of illustrators and themes. Pages
32-41 contain a valuable article by George Medhurst,
"British Paperback Fantasy 1941-6," reprinted from
Fantasy Commentator, Fall, 1946.

33. Owings, Mark and Jack L. Chalker. *The Index to the Science-Fantasy Publishers: A Bibliography of the Science Fiction and Fantasy Specialty Houses.* 2nd ed. Baltimore: The Anthem Series, 1966. 76pp. [paper].

The first published edition (all but a few copies of the first edition were destroyed by the publisher prior to distribution) of this annotated checklist of the science fiction and fantasy specialty publishers. Lists thirty-six publishers who produced only fantasy or science fiction titles (or non-fiction material relating to the genre) and issued at least one of them in hardcover format. Arranged alphabetically by publisher, with titles listed chronologically in order of publication; cross indexed by author and title. Short story collection and anthology contents are noted. The only comprehensive listing of the output of these specialty houses. A corrected and enlarged edition is needed.

34. Reginald, Robert. *Stella Nova: The Contemporary Science Fiction Authors.* Los Angeles: Unicorn & Son, 1970. Unpaged. [paper]. 2nd ed. New York: Arno Press, 1975 as *Contemporary Science Fiction Authors.* 368pp.

One of the most important recent science fiction checklists. The 1970 edition was not widely advertised and most copies were sold to public and institutional libraries. The second edition contains some corrections and amendments, but remains essentially the same as the original edition. The work includes 483 bibliographies of authors active during the period 1960-1968. Each entry provides a checklist of the author's science fiction and fantasy books listed in chronological order according to their sequence of publication. "A typical book entry contains the following information: identification number, year of publication, publisher, series number (where applicable), book title, and miscellaneous bibliographical information in parentheses, including type and format of each book, and some information regarding reprints." The checklist is arranged alphabetically by author. A title index and a list of pseudonyms is also provided. There are biographies of 308 of the authors indexed which often incorporate comments (sometimes lengthy) by writers responding to the compiler's questionnaire. This work is an absolutely essential reference tool for access to modern fantasy and science fiction titles.

35. Spelman, Richard C. *A Preliminary Checklist of Science Fiction and Fantasy Published by Ballantine Books (1953-1974)*. North Hollywood, CA: Institute for Specialized Literature, 1976. 42pp. [paper].

This work provides a preliminary listing of all fantasy and science fiction titles published by Ballantine Books through 1974 (though not so stated in the title or the foreword, most of the 1975 and some of the 1976 titles are included). The listing is by publisher's book number only--no access via author or title--thus the book's usefulness is severely limited. According to the compiler the work will be revised and expanded to cover the first twenty-five years of Ballantine Books, "perhaps in 1979 or 1980."

36. Spelman, Richard C. *Science Fiction and Fantasy Published by Ace Books (1953-1968)*. North Hollywood, CA: Institute for Specialized Literature, 1976. 62pp. [paper].

A useful checklist which lists A, D, F, G, H, K, M, N and S series by series number, and alphabetically by author and title.

37. Suvin, Darko. *Russian Science Fiction 1956-1974: A Bibliography*. Elizabethtown, NY: Dragon Press, 1976. 2nd ed. 73pp.

Originally published in Toronto in 1971, this second edition is an extended, enlarged and corrected version of the only English language checklist of modern Russian science fiction. The work is divided into three sections: SF books in the Russian language, 1956-1974; Russian SF in English and French books; and an annotated checklist of criticism published in books and periodicals in the Russian and English languages, 1956-1974. A selective checklist of critical works on Russian SF from the eighteenth century to 1956 is appendixed to the volume.

38. Tuck, Donald H. *The Encyclopedia of Science Fiction and Fantasy Through 1968. Volume 1: Who's Who, A-L*. Chicago: Advent, 1974. 286pp.

The culmination of over twenty years of research, this book is, in fact, the third edition of *A Handbook of Science Fiction and Fantasy* (see next entry). As of this writing, only the first (covering authors A-L and their works) of a projected three-volume series has appeared. The second volume will complete the author listings, while the third will include data on magazines, paperbacks, pseudonyms, connected stories, series and sequels, as well as details on

publishers, films, amateur magazines and other general
information. The author biographies and checklists
will comprise the principal portion of the *Encyclopedia*. "The basic idea of this section is to give the
user some indication of the different forms in which
a particular novel, collection, anthology, etc. has
appeared. The original title and presentation of the
item have been given as well as its appearances in
other forms and editions. . . . Pertinent nonfiction
is often separately covered, or at least mentioned
within the writer's biography." Full listings of the
contents of short story collections and anthologies
are an important feature, and this section covers
some 1550 single author collections and 950 anthologies (from the 1890s through 1968). Tuck stresses in
his introduction that this compilation compliments
the 1948 Bleiler *Checklist,* and "can be considered
as a sort of continuation to that book." Although the
author biographies and checklists are now nine years
out of date, the scope of this compilation is immense
and is likely to remain an important SF reference
tool for many years.

39. Tuck, Donald H. *A Handbook of Science Fiction and
    Fantasy.* Hobart, Tasmania: [Donald H. Tuck], 1954.
    151pp. [paper]; 2nd ed. Hobart, Tasmania: [Donald
    H. Tuck], 1959. 2 vols. 396pp. [paper].

These compilations are the basis for Tuck's *Encyclopedia of Science Fiction and Fantasy.* The 1959 edition
is partially superseded by the first volume of the
Encyclopedia. However, the second volume of this
edition will remain a valuable source until subsequent
volumes of the *Encyclopedia* are released. Coverage
includes listings of authors, with biographical and
bibliographical detail, editors, artists, persons of
note, fans, books, maps, films, societies, magazines;
a list of pseudonyms; an alphabetical guide to series,
serials, sequels, and connected stories; and an alphabetical list of paperback publications.

40. Whyte, Andrew Adams. *The New SF Bulletin: Index to SF
    Books 1974.* Boston: Paratime Press, 1974. 42pp.
    [paper].

Employs a special classification system with fourteen
categories to document science fiction first editions
and reprints published or announced for publication
in the United States in 1974.

(2) Subject Bibliographies

41. Carter, Margaret L. *Shadow of a Shade: A Survey of Vampirism in Literature*. (See III B2)

42. Clarke, Ignatius Frederick. *The Tale of the Future From the Beginning to the Present Day*. London: The Library Association, 1961. 165pp. 2nd ed. London: The Library Association, 1972. 196pp.

     The enlarged second edition is the standard work on the tale of the future, which comprises "those satires, ideal states, imaginary wars and invasions, political warnings and forecasts, interplanetary voyages and scientific romances--all located in an imaginary future period." The original edition contained approximately 1200 title entries. The enlarged edition was expanded to nearly 2300 entries. Entries are arranged in chronological sequence and cover works published between 1644 and 1970 in the United Kingdom. In addition to the main listing which briefly annotates each title, access is provided by author and title indices arranged in alphabetical sequence.

43. Clarke, I.F. *Voices Prophesying War 1763-1984*. (See III B2)

44. Eichner, Henry M. *Atlantean Chronicles*. (See III B2)

45. Gerber, Richard. *Utopian Fantasy*. (See III B2)

46. Gove, Philip Babcock. *The Imaginary Voyage in Prose Fiction*. (See III B2)

47. Locke, George. *Voyages in Space: A Bibliography of Interplanetary Fiction 1801-1914*. London: Ferret Fantasy, 1975. 80pp. [paper].

     Compiled by an antiquarian bookseller who spent many years collecting data on fantasy fiction, this work contains 263 fully annotated entries for books published in the English language before 1915 concerning interplanetary flight and/or descriptions of worlds other than Earth. Includes a statistical analysis of the books and an index of book and story titles, including those mentioned in the title abstracts.

48. Nicolson, Marjorie Hope. *Voyages to the Moon*. (See III B2)

49. Rabiega, William A. *Environmental Fiction for Pedagogic Purposes*. Monticello, IL: Council of Planning Librarians, 1974. Exchange Bibliography 590. 21pp. [paper].

An annotated bibliography of science fiction and fantasy novels and short stories with themes of ecology and environment, divided into four sections: environmental catastrophe, extraterrestrial environment, near future environment, and far future environment.

50. Roemer, Kenneth M. *The Obsolete Necessity: America in Utopian Writings, 1888-1900*. (See III B2)

51. Silverberg, Robert. *Drug Themes in Science Fiction*. Rockville, MD: National Institute on Drug Abuse, 1974. 55pp. [paper].

Includes a preface, introductory essay, and annotated checklist of approximately 75 novels and short stories with drug themes. The titles are arranged in chronological sequence in three sections: primitive period, c. 1900-1935; predictive period, c. 1935-1965; and contemporary period, c. 1965-1973. Indexed by author and title.

52. Summers, Alphonse Montague Joseph-Mary Augustus. *A Gothic Bibliography*. London: Fortune Press, 1941. 620pp. Rpt. New York: Russell & Russell, 1964.

The pioneer bibliography of the English Gothic novel from 1728 to 1916. A few French and German writers are included if their works were frequently translated into English or if they directly influenced the development of the Gothic novel in England. The volume is divided into two parts: the first, an index of authors providing biographical information and short title checklists of their works; the second, a partially annotated title index providing full bibliographic detail. This massive compilation remains the standard bibliographical study of English Gothic fiction.

53. Weinberg, Robert E. and Edward P. Berglund. *Reader's Guide to the Cthulhu Mythos*. rev. ed. Albuquerque: Silver Scarab Press, 1973. 88pp.

This comprehensive checklist is an enlargement of Weinberg's *A Reader's Guide to the Cthulhu Mythos* published in 1969, and cites published and unpublished fiction, poetry, and non-fiction utilizing or commenting on the mythos. Organized into the following sections: chronological listing by publication dates; alphabetical listing by title; alphabetical listing by author; series listing; alphabetical listing by author of non-fiction; alphabetical listing by author of parodies; alphabetical listing by author of poetry; alphabetical listing by author of books, pamphlets, brochures, etc.; and non-English publications.

(3) Anthology Indices

54. Cole, Walter R. *A Checklist of Science-Fiction
    Anthologies.* [Brooklyn, NY: W.R. Cole, 1964].
    374pp. Rpt. New York: Arno Press, 1975.

    A checklist of approximately 260 English language
    anthologies of fantasy and science fiction published
    between 1927 and 1963. Entries are indexed alphabe-
    tically by anthology title; by editor (this section
    provides bibliographical data and a complete listing
    of contents for each entry); by story title; and by
    contributing author. The 1962-63 listings are appen-
    ded. Still the basic source for anthologized fantasy
    and science fiction, though an update is needed. Re-
    searchers are advised that *An Index to Science Fiction
    Anthologies and Collections* by William G. Contento,
    listing approximately 1900 anthologies and single
    author story collections published through June 1977,
    will be issued by G.K. Hall in 1978.

55. New England Science Fiction Association. (See II B4a)

56. Siemon, Frederick. *Science Fiction Story Index:
    1950-1968.* Chicago: American Library Association,
    1971. 275pp. [paper].

    A listing of approximately 3400 stories, indexed by
    author and title and keyed to the anthologies and
    single author collections in which they appear. An
    incomplete work which is difficult to use and often
    provides unreliable information.

(4) Magazine Indices

a. General

57. Australian Science Fiction Association. *Index to
    British Science Fiction Magazines: 1934-1953.*
    7 vols. Canberra City: Australian Science Fiction
    Association, [1968?]-1975. [34], [60], [70], [82],
    [42], [48], [36]pp. [paper].

    Indexes British SF magazines, including British ed-
    itions of titles published in the United States. The
    format for this compilation is superior to that of
    Donald B. Day's more inclusive *Index to the Science-
    Fiction Magazines: 1926-1950,* as each magazine entry
    provides a listing of contents. The following maga-
    zines are indexed: *Scoops, Tales of Wonder, Fantasy,*

*Astounding Science Fiction, Science Fiction, Future
Fiction, Science Fiction Quarterly, Dynamic Science
Fiction, Yankee Science Fiction, The Moon Conquerors,
Into the Fourth Dimension, Space-Fact and Fiction,
Strange Tales, Thrilling Stories, New Worlds* (1-21),
Science-Fantasy (1-6), *Amazing Stories, Fantastic Ad-
ventures, Fantastic Strange Adventures, Futuristic
Stories, Thrilling Wonder Stories, Fantasy* (2nd ser-
ies), *Startling Stories, Cosmic Science Stories,
Super Science Stories, Planet Stories, Fantastic
Novels, Worlds at War, Worlds of Fantasy, Futuristic
Science Stories, Tales of Tomorrow, Wonders of the
Spaceways, Authentic Science Fiction* (1-40), *Nebula
Science Fiction, Marvell Science Stories, Space Sci-
ence Stories, Galaxy Science Fiction* (1-8), *Magazine
of Fantasy and Science Fiction* (1-12) and *If* (1-15).
A brief history of the British SF magazine is also
provided.

58. Cockcroft, Thomas G.L. *Index to Fiction in Radio News
and Other Magazines*. Lower Hutt, New Zealand: T.G.L.
Cockcroft, 1970. 12pp. [paper].

This index is based primarily on previous lists, *The
Gernsback Forerunners,* compiled by William H. Evans
(Brooklyn: Julius Unger, 1944?) and Theodore Engel's
compilation checklist which occupied most of a booklet, *Evolution of Modern Science Fiction,* published
by Hugo Gernsback in 1952. Fiction, as well as some
articles and plays, is indexed by author and title.
Magazines indexed are: *Modern Electrics, Practical
Electrics, The Experimenter, Radio News, The Electri-
cal Experimenter,* and *Science and Invention.*

59. Cockcroft, Thomas G.L. *Index to the Weird Fiction
Magazines.* Lower Hutt, New Zealand: T.G.L. Cockcroft, 1962-1964. 2 vols. 55, [47]pp. [paper].
Rev. ed., 1967 [paper]. Rpt. New York: Arno Press,
1975. 2 vols. in 1.

Indexes the contents of fantasy and adventure pulps
by author and title. Includes *Weird Tales, Strange
Stories, Strange Tales, The Thrill Book, Oriental
Stories, The Magic Carpet Magazine, Strange Tales*
(British), and *Golden Fleece.*

60. Day, Bradford M. *The Complete Checklist of Science-
Fiction Magazines.* Woodhaven, NY: Science-Fiction
and Fantasy Publications, 1961. 63pp. [paper].

A comprehensive checklist of over 200 English and
foreign language magazines whose contents were devoted to or emphasized fantastic fiction (including
fantasy, science-fantasy, weird, weird mystery,

horror, occult, erotica, historical fantasy, adventure, etc.). Covers the period 1895 (commencing
chronologically with the general fiction magazine
Black Cat) to 1960. Lists magazine titles, issues
published, and magazine type only; contents are not
provided. Some errors and omissions were corrected
in a six-page supplement issued in 1964. Still an
essential reference tool.

61. Day, Bradford M. *An Index on the Weird & Fantastica
    in Magazines*. South Ozone Park, NY: Bradford M.
    Day, 1953. 162pp. [paper].

    Chronological checklists comprising: a complete list-
    ing of contents issue by issue of *Weird Tales* (thru
    November 1953), *Golden Fleece, Strange Tales, Oriental
    Stories, Magic Carpet, Tales of Magic and Mystery,
    The Thrill Book,* and *Strange Stories*; lists of the
    fantasy stories from *Complete Stories, Romance Maga-
    zine, Popular Magazine, The Idler, Blue Book,* and
    eight Frank A. Munsey publications (*All-American
    Fiction, All-Story Magazine, The Argosy, The Cavalier,
    Live Wire, Munsey's Magazine, Ocean,* and *Scrap Book*),
    as well as incomplete lists for *Adventure, Black Book
    Detective, Cosmopolitan, Everybody's Magazine, Top
    Notch,* and eight others; and "A Checklist of Fantas-
    tic Magazines," which was expanded and published in
    1961 as *The Complete Checklist of Science-Fiction
    Magazines* (see II B4a).

62. Day, Donald B. *Index to the Science-Fiction Magazines
    1926-1950*. Portland, OR: Perri Press, 1952. 184pp.

    Indexes the contents of 58 science fiction magazines
    from their first issues through December 1950. Only
    English language magazines are covered, and with the
    exception of three British titles (*Fantasy, New
    Worlds,* and *Tales of Wonder*), all are U.S. publica-
    tions. Indexed alphabetically by author and title,
    with a separate checklist of magazines indexed chron-
    ologically by issue. A pioneer effort which remains
    the standard index for SF magazines of the period.

63. Gernsback, Hugo. *Evolution of Modern Science Fiction*.
    [New York: Hugo Gernsback, 1952]. 12pp. [paper].

    Pages 3-12 comprise a chronological checklist compiled
    by Theodore Engel of science fiction published in
    Gernsback magazines from 1911 through 1928. Publica-
    tions indexed include *Modern Electrics, Electrical
    Experimenter, Science and Invention, Radio News,
    Practical Electrics,* and *The Experimenter*.

64. Jones, Robert Kenneth. "Popular's Weird Menace Pulps:
Essay and Index." In *The Weird Menace*. Evergreen,
CO: Opar Press, 1972. [60]pp. [paper].

A brief history of the weird menace pulps is followed
by a list of fiction, arranged alphabetically by auth-
or, appearing in *Dime Mystery, Horror Stories, Terror
Tales, Sinister Stories, Startling Mystery,* and *Thrilling Mystery.*

65. Metcalf, Norm. *The Index of Science Fiction Magazines
1951-1965.* El Cerrito, CA: J. Ben Stark, 1968.
253pp. [paper].

Indexes approximately 100 English language magazines
(mostly SF, but a few fantasy titles are included),
alphabetically by author and by title. Includes a
separate checklist of magazines indexed as well as
a list of editors.

66. New England Science Fiction Association. *Index to the
Science Fiction Magazines 1966-1970.* Cambridge, MA:
New England Science Fiction Association, 1971.
82pp. *The N.E.S.F.A. Index. Science Fiction Maga-
zines: 1971-1972 and Original Anthologies: 1971-
1972.* Cambridge, MA: NESFA, 1973. 42pp. [paper].
*The N.E.S.F.A. Index. Science Fiction Magazines
[1973]: and Original Anthologies [1973].* Cambridge,
MA: NESFA, 1974. 30pp. [paper]. *The N.E.S.F.A
Index to the Science Fiction Magazines and Original
Anthologies 1974.* Cambridge, MA: NESFA, 1975. 43pp.
[paper]. *The N.E.S.F.A. Index: Science Fiction Magazines and Original Anthologies 1975.* Cambridge,
MA: NESFA, 1976. 36pp. [paper].

The five-year index compiled by Anthony Lewis includes
all of the U.S. and British science fiction magazines
published during the period 1966-1970. Intended as a
continuation of the *Index to the Science Fiction Magazines, 1951-1965,* compiled by Erwin S. Strauss (see
II B4a), and following the triple listing format (by
magazine, by story title, and by author). Commencing
with the 1971-1972 supplement, coverage was extended
to include original anthologies. Anthony Lewis continued to compile the magazine information, while
Andrew A. Whyte assumed responsibility for the anthologies. Offset from computer printout.

67. Pavlat, Robert amd William Evans, eds. *Fanzine Index
. . . Listing Most Fanzines From the Beginning
Through 1952 Including Titles, Editors' Names and
Data on Each Issue.* Flushing, NY: Harold Palmer
Piser, 1965. 143pp. [paper].

Originally issued in five fascicles between December
1952 and November 1959, this index, the most extensive
listing of amateur journals of this type issued to
date, is based on the earlier research of R.D. Swisher
on fanzines from their beginnings in 1930 through
mid-1946, with subsequent information provided by
Pavlat, Evans, and others. The compilation is arranged alphabetically by title and includes listings of
editors, volume and issue numbers, dates, size, number of pages, and reproduction method. An essential
reference tool.

68. Roberts, Peter. *Peter Roberts' Little Gem Guide to
    SF Fanzines*. London: Peter Roberts, 1974. [10]pp.
    [paper].

A concise listing of limited scope compiled to intro-
duce new fans to SF amateur publications. Of some
value for its information on foreign, especially UK,
fanzines.

69. Stone, Graham. *Australian Science Fiction Index 1925-
    1967*. Canberra City: Australian Science Fiction
    Association, [1968]. 158pp. [paper].

A revised and enlarged version of Stone's *Australian
Science Fiction Index 1939-1962,* issued in 1964 by
the Futurian Society of Sydney. This compilation indexes all of the fantasy and science fiction published
in hard-cover books, paperbacks, and magazines in
Australia, from Erle Cox's *Out of the Silence* through
1967. Indexes the following magazines and series in
chronological sequence: *Thrills Incorporated, Future
Science Fiction, Popular Science Fiction, Orbit Science Fiction, The Magazine of Fantasy and Science
Fiction* (Australian ed.)*, Selected Science Fiction
Magazine, Science-Fiction Monthly, Science Fiction
Library, Satellite Series, Scientific Thriller, Fantasy Fiction,* and *American Science Fiction.* Magazine
and series contents are cross-indexed by author and
by title.

70. Strauss, Erwin S. *The MIT Science Fiction Society's
    Index to the S-F Magazines, 1951-1965.* Cambridge,
    MA: The MIT Science Fiction Society, 1965. 207pp.

Indexes the contents of 100 English language fantasy
and science fiction magazines for the period 1951-1965
chronologically by magazine issue and alphabetically
by author and by title. Entries were arranged by computer and the volume is photo-offset from the printout.

71. Weinberg, Robert and Lohr McKinstry. *The Hero Pulp Index*. rev. ed. Evergreen, CO: Opar Press, 1971. 48pp. [paper].

A revision of the original version of this index published by Weinberg in 1970. Lists fiction featuring 56 characters from the "hero pulps." The main section arranges the heroes alphabetically and lists the principal novel in each pulp in which they are featured. Other sections provide information on series authors, pen names, reprints, and brief sketches of the fictional heroes. In addition to the heroes working within the fantasy genre, the index covers those in specialty adventure pulps (i.e., *Bill Barnes, Air Adventurer*) as well as the detective and the western genres.

b. Individual

72. Cazedessus, C.E., Jr., ed. *Ghost Stories*. . . Evergreen, CO: Opar Press, 1973. 32pp. [paper].

The main feature is an author/title index of fiction and articles published in *Ghost Stories* (1926-1932) compiled by James Sieger. Appendices include listing of editorial staff, magazine departments and features, cover artists, and reprint editions. Sam Moskowitz provides a historical essay, "Neglected Repository of Supernatural Fiction."

73. Eisgruber, Frank, Jr. *Gangland's Doom: The Shadow of the Pulps*. (See III B4b)

74. Hoffman, Stuart. *An Index to* Unknown *and* Unknown Worlds *by Author and by Title*. Black Earth, WI: Sirius Press, 1955. 34pp. [paper].

Indexes the contents of *Unknown* and *Unknown Worlds* alphabetically by author and by title. The locale and principal characters of each story are listed.

75. New England Science Fiction Association. *Index to Perry Rhodan--American Edition*. 2 vols. Cambridge, MA: NESFA, 1973-1975. 12, 18pp. [paper].

An index of this serial publication with listing by issue arranged chronologically as well as alphabetically by title and author, compiled by Anthony R. Lewis.

76. Okada, Masaya. *Illustrated Index to Air Wonder Stories (Vol. 1 No. 1--Vol. 1 No. 11 July 1929--May 1930)*. Nagoya, Japan: Masaya Okada, 1973. 79pp. [paper].

Indexed by magazine issue, by author, and by title. Also indexes the various features and departments. The cover and principal interior illustrations are well produced on coated stock.

(5) Film

77. Lee, Walt. *Reference Guide to Fantastic Films: Science Fiction, Fantasy & Horror*. 3 vols. Los Angeles: Chelsea-Lee Books, 1972-1974. 81, 559, 80, 38, 14pp. [paper].

The single most valuable work on the fantastic cinema. Lists 20,000 titles, covering every science fiction, horror, fantasy, animated, and borderline film that Lee could find reference to. Each entry provides technical information, including director and cast, notation of content, and references to reviews. Covers films produced in approximately fifty countries over a seventy-five year period.

78. Willis, Donald C. *Horror and Science Fiction Films: A Checklist*. Metuchen, NJ: Scarecrow Press, 1972. 612pp.

Some 4,400 titles are included in this compilation of science fiction and horror movie data. Comprehensive production data, full credits, and a lively synopsis and commentary are provided for the obscure and the well-known, and for the worst as well as the best of horror and SF films.

III. SOURCES FOR SECONDARY MATERIALS

A. GENERAL

79. *British Humanities Index* [1962-]. London: Library
    Association, 1963- .

    A continuation of the now defunct *Subject Index to
    Periodicals* (1915-1962), which indexes primarily
    British and American periodicals. Because of its
    coverage of over 250 British periodicals, BHI is a
    necessary supplement to the *Social Sciences and
    Humanities Index*. Quarterly issues are arranged by
    subject only; the annual issues add an author section.

80. *Dissertation Abstracts International*. Ann Arbor, MI:
    University Microfilms, 1938- .

    Formerly *Dissertation Abstracts,* a compilation of
    abstracts of dissertations submitted to University
    Microfilms by a varying number of cooperating uni-
    versities. The main list is arranged by subject
    field and then by university. Author and subject
    indices. Issued monthly.

81. *Education Index* [1929-]. New York: Wilson, 1932- .

    A subject index to 240 periodicals in the field of
    education. Issued monthly except for July and August.

82. English Association. *The Year's Work in English
    Studies* [1919-]. London: Oxford University
    Press, 1921- .

    A selective, critical survey of studies of English
    literature appearing in books and articles published
    in Britain, Europe, and the United States, grouped by
    chronological periods. Covers much the same ground as
    the MHRA *Annual Bibliography*, but providing running
    comment on a work's importance or character.

83. *Essay and General Literature Index, 1900-1933*.
    New York: Wilson, 1934. Supplementary volumes,
    New York: Wilson, 1934- .

An index to essays and articles published in collections since 1900. Arranged by author, title, and subject. Semi-annual and annual accumulations.

84. *Humanities Index*. New York: Wilson, 1974- .

Continues in part the *Social Science and Humanities Index* (which see). Quarterly, with annual accumulations.

85. *Library Literature* [1921/32-]. New York: Wilson, 1934- .

An index to current books, pamphlets, and articles relating to librarianship. International in scope, some 160 journals are covered. Arranged by author and subject; issued bimonthly with an annual accumulation.

86. McNamee, Lawrence F. *Dissertations in English and American Literature: Theses Accepted by American, British and German Universities, 1865-1964*. New York: Bowker, 1968.

Dissertations are listed in a subject arrangement which includes chapters on the teaching of English, literary periods, genres, individual authors, etc. Index of authors of dissertations. A more complete work than *Dissertation Abstracts International*. Supplements 1-2 provide coverage for the period 1964-73.

87. *Masters Abstracts*. Ann Arbor: University Microfilms, 1962- .

Abstracts of selected M.A. theses from American universities.

88. Modern Humanities Research Association. *Annual Bibliography of English Language and Literature* [1920-]. Cambridge, England: Cambridge University Press, 1921- .

An annual list of English and American literature, including books, pamphlets, and periodical articles, with references to reviews of books listed. Broader in scope than *Year's Work in English Studies,* although not as complete as the *MLA International Bibliography*. Arranged by subject in the language section and chronologically in the literature section.

89. Modern Language Association of America. *MLA International Bibliography of Books and Articles on the Modern Languages and Literatures*. New York: Modern Language Association of America, 1921- .

Now published separately from its parent journal *PMLA* in four volumes. Volume I is a listing of literary studies. Coverage is international, and is divided into special topics, periods, and genres. Issued annually to MLA members.

90. *Reader's Guide to Periodical Literature* [1900-   ].
    Minneapolis (later New York): Wilson, 1901-   .

    Begun as an index that included only fifteen periodicals, it assimilated the *Cumulative Index* in 1903 and the *American Library Index* in 1911. In 1953 it expanded still further to include many American periodicals of a popular nature. Arranged by author, title, and subject.

91. *Research in Education*. Washington: U.S. Department of
    Health, Education and Welfare, 1966-   .

    Title changed to *Resources in Education* in 1975. Lists and provides resumes of educational research reports and scholarly papers and addresses of interest to the educational community. A reference source for unpublished papers. Beginning in 1968, semi-annual and annual accumulated indices to subject and author are available.

92. *Social Science and Humanities Index*. New York: Wilson,
    1965- 1973.

    A continuation of the *International Index to Periodicals* (1907-1965). An index to British and American articles, with a more scholarly emphasis than the *Reader's Guide*. Arranged by subjects that conform to the American Library Association and the Library of Congress subject headings. In 1974, SSHI was split into separate indices: *Humanities Index* and *Social Sciences Index*.

93. *Social Sciences Index*. New York: Wilson, 1974-   .

    Continues in part the *Social Sciences and Humanities Index* (which see). Quarterly, with annual accumulations.

   B. SCIENCE FICTION

      (1) General Bibliographies

94. Barron, Neil, ed. *Anatomy of Wonder*. (See II Bl)

95. Clareson, Thomas D. *Science Fiction Criticism: An Annotated Checklist*. [Kent, OH]: Kent State University Press, 1972. 225pp.

A comprehensive guide to the critical literature on the SF genre published in English language books and periodicals prior to 1972. Contains approximately 800 annotated entries arranged in nine sections: General Studies; Literary Studies; Book Reviews; The Visual Arts; Futurology, Utopia and Dystopia; Classroom and Library; Publishing; Specialist Bibliographies, Checklists and Indices; and The Contemporary Scene. Indexed by author only.

(2) Subject Studies & Bibliographies

96. Atkinson, Geoffroy. *The Extraordinary Voyage in French Literature Before 1700*. New York: Columbia University Press, 1920. 189pp. *The Extraordinary Voyage in French Literature From 1700 to 1720*. Paris: Librairie Ancienne Honore Champion, 1922. 147pp. [paper].

Atkinson's valuable works comprise the first detailed twentieth-century contributions to the study of the French imaginary voyage through 1720. Following a general discussion of the extraordinary voyage and its antecedents are detailed analyses of *La Terre Australe Connue* by Gabriel Foigny, *L'Histoire des Sevarambes* by Denis Vairasse d'Alais, *Historie de Calejava* by Claude Gilbert, *Voyage de Groenland* by Simon Tyssot, and other works. Includes valuable appendices and bibliographies.

97. Berger, Harold L. *Science Fiction and the New Dark Age*. Bowling Green, OH: Bowling Green University Popular Press, 1976. 231pp.

A study of the anti-utopian trend in contemporary science fiction organized into twelve thematic units: The Hostility to Science, Man Versus Machine, The Synthetic Experience, Ignoble Utopias, The Totalitarian State of the Future, The Mind Invasion, Commerce and Exploitation, The Revolt of Youth, Nuclear War, The Population Explosion, Race War in America, The Obsessional Catastrophe. Provides a wide-ranging and detailed examination of works, several of which have hithertofore received little critical attention. Includes a bibliography of approximately 160 fiction and non-fiction titles germane to the study.

25

98. Carter, Margaret L. *Shadow of a Shade: A Survey of Vampirism in Literature*. New York: Gordon Press, 1975. 176pp.

A historical survey of vampire literature in the English language with emphasis on the British tradition. Except for Poe and Lovecraft, there is little commentary on the theme in American literature prior to the 1940s. Textual references and notes are sparse, and the bibliography is often inadequately referenced (many book entries lack notations of publisher and date, while periodical entries often lack issue number and/or date as well as page references). Regardless of these drawbacks, part four of the bibliography, "Stories of Vampirism," provides a useful checklist of nearly 350 tales appearing in English language books and magazines. The publisher has done Carter a grave disservice in that the book is poorly reproduced from the original typescript (complete with hundreds of strikeovers) and moreover suffers from lack of editorial control and proofreading. Nonetheless, this work should be consulted by those researching this theme.

99. Clarke, I[gnatius] F. *Voices Prophesying War 1763-1984*. London: Oxford University Press, 1966. 254pp.

The pioneering study of the literature of futuristic wars and war technology. Includes a wide variety of "fiction," such as propaganda, contemporary war accounts, comments on the nature of war, and discussion of war's aftermath. The definitive study of the future war motif in European fiction. Appended to the study are useful bibliographies, including a "Select List of War Studies, 1770-1964," which lists works on the theory and practice of war, and "Check List of Imaginary Wars, 1763-1965," which comprises the most extensive listing of imaginary war fiction (in English, French and German) published to date.

100. De Camp, L. Sprague and George H. Scithers, eds. *The Conan Grimore*. Baltimore: Mirage Press, 1972. 263pp.

Material on the sword-and-sorcery literary tradition with emphasis on the work of Robert E. Howard and his influence on this sub-genre. The 35 essays, articles, fictions, and poems are reprinted from *Arma,* an important amateur magazine founded in 1956 with the work of Howard and his

literary successors as the focal point. Contributors
include Howard (letters, book review, and a fragment),
Fritz Leiber, de Camp, Poul Anderson, E. Hoffman
Price, and Jerry Pournelle. Subjects include Howard
and his writings, E.R. Addison, Jack Vance, Talbot
Mundy, Leiber, etc.

101. De Camp, L. Sprague. *The Conan Reader*. Baltimore:
     Mirage Press, 1968. 149pp.

     Thirteen essays and articles reprinted from *Arma*
     with emphasis on Conan and his creator, Robert E.
     Howard. Other subjects include Dunsany, Conan's
     imitators, and Fletcher Pratt's fantasy fiction.
     Pages 94-148 comprise a dictionary of Hyborian
     people and place names. De Camp has edited and
     completed Howard's Conan tales as well as adding
     new ones to the canon.

102. De Camp, L. Sprague. *The Conan Swordbook: 27 Exam-
     inations of Heroic Fiction*. Baltimore: Mirage
     Press, 1969. 259pp.

     Essays and articles on heroic fantasy with emphasis
     on the sword and sorcery writing of Robert E. Howard,
     selected from early issues of *Arma*. Similar in scope
     and format to *The Conan Grimore* (which see). Contri-
     butors include Howard (letters), Poul Anderson, Glenn
     Lord, de Camp (on editing Conan), Fritz Leiber, Mar-
     ion Zimmer Bradley, and Leigh Brackett. Subjects in-
     clude Howard and his life and writings, E.R. Eddison,
     Edgar Rice Burroughs, James Branch Cabell, and T.H.
     White.

103. Eichner, Henry M. *Atlantean Chronicles*. Alhambra,
     CA: Fantasy Publishing Company, 1971. 230pp.

     An informal study of theories concerning the location
     of Atlantis. The bibliography, which comprises the
     final 99 pages of the volume, is the most extensive
     listing to date of the Atlantis theme in fiction.
     The core is an annotated listing, with detailed plot
     summaries, of over 130 English language novels. In
     addition, there are non-annotated checklists of
     fiction appearing in *Amazing Stories* and *Weird Tales*;
     foreign language works; and secondary materials.

104. Elliott, Robert C. *The Shape of Utopia: Studies in
     a Literary Genre*. Chicago and London: University
     of Chicago Press, 1970. 158pp.

     A collection of seven essays published by the author
     in various academic journals. The essays deal with

the utopian genre itself--its characteristics and
purposes--and with individual literary utopias.
Elliott concludes that "our writers no longer create
imaginative versions of the ideal society with the
easy confidence of the nineteenth century."

105. Eurich, Nell. *Science in Utopia: A Mighty Design.*
     Cambridge, MA: Harvard University Press, 1967.
     332pp.

The emphasis in this study is on 17th century science
and its influence on utopian literature. The final
chapter relates the earlier tradition to that of the
20th century, pointing out that science, reflected
in the utopian writings of the 17th century, offered
its greatest hope for mankind; while modern dystopian
writings show science used to control the individual.

106. Gerber, Richard. *Utopian Fantasy: A Study of English
     Utopian Fiction Since the End of the Nineteenth
     Century.* London: Routledge & Kegan Paul, 1955.
     162pp. Rpt. [Folcroft, PA: Folcroft Press, n.d.];
     [2nd ed.] New York: McGraw-Hill, 1973. 168pp.
     [paper].

A study of the basic themes and forms of modern
utopian fiction beginning with the rise of the
basic modern utopian attitude, "the belief in the
. . . power of unlimited . . . pogress," and culminating in the sophisticated nightmares of Aldous
Huxley and George Orwell. Contains "An Annotated
List of English Utopian Fantasies 1901-1951," which
has been extended to 1971 in the second edition.

107. Gibson, R.W. *St. Thomas More: A Preliminary Bibli-
     ography of his Works and Moreana to the Year 1750
     . . . With a Bibliography of Utopiana Compiled by
     R.W. Gibson and J. Max Patrick.* (See IV B)

108. Glut, Donald F. *The Dracula Book.* Metuchen, NJ:
     Scarecrow Press, 1975. 388pp.

A sketch of the vampire in Western tradition and
its manifestation in the arts via the Dracula
legend. Includes commentary on other Dracula books,
vampires on television and in comic strips, and
in film.

109. Glut, Donald F. *The Frankenstein Legend: A Tribute
     to Mary Shelley and Boris Karloff.* Metuchen, NJ:
     Scarecrow Press, 1973. 372pp.

The story of the Frankenstein monster in legend,
literature, theater, motion pictures, television,
radio, and comic books.

110. Gove, Philip Babcock. *The Imaginary Voyage in Prose
     Fiction. A History of Its Criticism and a Guide
     for Its Study, with an Annotated Check List of
     215 Imaginary Voyages from 1700 to 1800*. New York:
     Columbia University Press, 1941. 445pp.   Rpt.
     New York: Arno Press, 1975.

     A history of the criticism of the imaginary voyage,
     "including discussion of definitions, history of
     the use of the term, the Robinsonade, and the re-
     lationship of the imaginary voyage to other forms
     of prose fiction." Part Two "provides an extensive
     annotated bibliography of 215 imaginary voyages
     published between 1700 and 1800. Also included are
     a bibliography of works consulted, and an index of
     subjects, authors, and titles mentioned in the text.
     Gove's book is the classic treatment of this rela-
     tively unknown field."

111. Green, Roger Lancelyn. *Into Other Worlds: Space-
     Flight in Fiction, from Lucian to Lewis*. London
     and New York: Abelard-Schuman, 1957. 190pp.
     Rpt. New York: Arno Press, 1975.

     "An attempt to describe the outstanding journeys to
     the Moon and the planets in the writings of story-
     tellers from Lucian the Greek near the beginning of
     the Christian era, to those of . . . C.S. Lewis."
     Liberal quotations from the texts of the books are
     used to supplement the sparse historical commentary.
     Contains "A Short Bibliography of Journeys into
     Other Worlds, Mentioned in this Book" covering the
     period 1634 to 1943.

112. Hillegas, Mark R. *The Future as Nightmare: H.G.
     Wells and the Anti-Utopians*. New York: Oxford
     University Press, 1967. 200pp.   Rpt. Carbondale:
     Southern Illinois University Press, 1974.

     The first systematic study of 20th century anti-
     utopian fiction. Hillegas examines Wells' "Huxleyan
     pessimism" in a lucid discussion of his scientific
     romances, utopias and future histories, and traces
     their influence upon the "admonitory satires,"
     Forster's "The Machine Stops," Zamyatin's *We*, Hux-
     ley's *Brave New World*, Orwell's *1984*, Capek's *RUR*,
     and Lewis' trilogy, *Out of the Silent Planet, Pere-
     landra*, and *That Hideous Strength*. Final chapters
     deal with other anti-utopian works emerging from the
     literary mainstream and from the sf pulps of the 1950s.

113. Leighton, Peter. *Moon Travellers: A Dream that is Becoming a Reality*. London: Oldbourne, 1960. 240pp.

Following a brief two-chapter survey of pre-20th century imaginary lunar voyages, this work concentrates on Lucian's *True History*; Kepler's *Dream About the Moon*; Godwin's *Man in the Moon*; Wilkins' *Discovery of a New World*; Cyrano de Bergerac's *Voyage to the Moon*; Defoe's *The Consolidator*; Brunt's *A Voyage to Cacklogallinia*; Locke's "Moon Hoax"; Poe's "Hans Pfaall"; Verne's *From the Earth to the Moon*; and Wells' *The First Men in the Moon*. Additional works are briefly mentioned. Interpretive commentary is slight, with the bulk of the work comprising summaries and liberal quotations from these works. A bibliography of works cited is included.

114. McNutt, Daniel J. *The Eighteenth-Century Gothic Novel: An Annotated Bibliography of Criticism and Selected Texts*. New York and London: Garland Publishing, 1975. 330pp.

Presently the most complete bibliography of scholarship devoted to the 18th century Gothic novel. The thirteen chapters comprise: bibliographies and research guides; aesthetic background; literary background; psychological, social, and scientific background; eighteenth-century Gothic; the Gothic legacy; Horace Walpole; Clara Reeve; Charlotte Smith; Ann Radcliffe; Matthew Gregory Lewis; and William Beckford. The more than 1000 annotated entries range from early reviews to modern scholarship. Emphasis is on English language material, but selected foreign language items are listed in the appendix. The extensive chapters on individual authors provide details on selected texts, bibliographies, full-length studies, articles, essays, introductions, notices in general works, diaries, and early reviews.

115. Nicolson, Marjorie Hope. *Voyages to the Moon*. New York: Macmillan, 1948. 297pp.

A standard source for analysis and summary of the pre-nineteenth century cosmic voyage "*as English readers knew it* in the seventeenth and eighteenth centuries." Emphasis is on the English voyage, with treatment of the motif in Europe limited, with a few exceptions, to those mentioned in an English book. The final chapter analyzes the debt of Poe, Verne, Wells and Lewis to their literary predecessors. Appended is an important annotated bibliography of the literature of imaginary flight, plus a checklist of secondary material.

116. Parrington, Vernon Louis. *American Dreams: A Study of American Utopias*. Providence, RI: Brown University Press, 1947. 234pp. 2nd ed. New York: Russell & Russell, 1864. 246pp.

The title is somewhat misleading, as this is a study of American literary utopias. The pioneer study of this theme and, while a few important early American novels are overlooked, it remains the most comprehensive work of its type. Emphasis is on late 19th century fiction, with the chapter, "Mars and Utopia," of special interest to students of science fiction. Includes a brief, partially annotated bibliography of utopian fiction and tracts published between 1659 and 1946 arranged in chronological sequence. The second edition adds a chapter, "Dystopias and Utopias--A Postscript," which discusses the post-war utopia and dystopia.

117. Roemer, Kenneth M. *The Obsolete Necessity: America in Utopian Writings, 1888-1890*. [Kent, OK]: Kent State University Press, 1976. 239pp.

An examination of the vast body of late 19th century utopian and anti-utopian literature in its historical context and in terms of the perennial American ideal of progress and change. A meticulous analysis of 160 works published in the U.S. from post-Bellamy to the end of the century. Includes an annotated bibliography, the most extensive published to date, of American utopian fiction issued between 1888 and 1900.

118. Walsh, Chad. *From Utopia to Nightmare*. New York and Evanston: Harper & Row, 1962. 191pp. Rpt. Westport, CT: Greenwood Press, 1972.

A study of the gradual decline of the utopian novel and its displacement by the dystopian or "inverted utopia." Deals only briefly with the utopia; the focus is on the dystopia, which manifests itself as a literary reaction to Bellamy's *Looking Backward* (1888). Analyzes works against their historical and ideological background, noting not only the passing of the utopian vision but also of humanism "before the diverse forces of the 20th century."

119. Weinberg, Robert E. and Edward P. Berglund. *Reader's Guide to the Cthulhu Mythos*. Albuquerque: Silver Scarab Press, 1973. 88pp. [paper].

The enlarged second edition of *A Reader's Guide to the Cthulhu Mythos* by Rovert Weinberg (1969). The

most comprehensive checklist of the "Mythos" tales
by Lovecraft and others, including much fiction
only remotely connected with the theme. Indexed
chronologically with an alphabetical cross index.
Includes series listing; separate listings of non-
fiction, parodies, and poetry; foreign editions in
English and other languages; and books and pamphlets arranged alphabetically by title. No general
index.

(3) General Surveys & Histories

120. Aldiss, Brian W. *Billion Year Spree: The History
     of Science Fiction*. London: Weidenfeld & Nicol-
     son, 1973. 339pp.

     A general critical survey of the genre by a leading
     writer of science fiction. Aldiss contends that
     science fiction "was born in the heart of the Eng-
     lish Romantic movement with Mary Shelley's *Franken-
     stein*" and devotes the whole of his first chapter
     to establishing this argument. The book's eleven
     chapters are divided equally between the 19th and
     20th centuries, with a single chapter devoted to
     the precursors of science fiction. The chapter on
     John W. Campbell and the *Astounding* era is probably
     the most well-balanced and well-developed, while
     the last two chapters, which deal with the 1950s
     and beyond, are sketchy and pass too quickly over
     some of the important writers and works of the
     post-World War II period.

121. Amis, Kingsley. *New Maps of Hell: A Survey of
     Science Fiction*. New York: Harcourt, Brace,
     1960. 161pp. Rpt. New York: Arno Press, 1975.

     The first full-length study of the genre by a
     critic from outside the science fiction community.
     This study "gave direction to current criticism
     of science fiction by emphasizing its role 'as an
     instrument of social diagnosis and warning.'"
     Text is based upon a series of lectures given by
     Amis at Princeton University during 1958-59.

122. Armytage, W.H.G. *Yesterday's Tomorrows: A Historical
     Survey of Future Societies*. London: Routledge &
     Kegan Paul, 1968. 288pp.

     This well-documented study illustrates how, "out of
     the long process of preparatory day-dreams, imagined
     encounters, wish-fulfillments, and compensatory

projections, a constructive debate about tomorrow is emerging," providing man with material to evaluate his needs for the future. Copious notes and references to hundreds of titles enhance the value of this essential background work.

123. Ash, Brian. *Faces of the Future: The Lessons of Science Fiction.* London: Elek Books, 1975. 213pp.

The author reviews a wide-ranging selection of SF works to provide an informal, loosely-constructed account of the development of modern science fiction in its broadest aspects. Critical commentary is slight; a good general introduction to the field and more thorough than Sam Lundwall's *Science Fiction: What It's All About* (which see).

124. Bailey, J.O. *Pilgrims Through Space and Time: Trends and Patterns in Scientific and Utopian Fiction.* New York: Argus Books, 1947. 341pp. Rpt. Westport, CT: Greenwood Press, 1972.

The pioneer critical study of the scientific and utopian romance in English. Emphasis is on fiction published prior to 1914. Still a standard work, its chief value being the thematic arrangement of the material. Divided into two parts: the first, a chronological survey subdivided into historical periods with treatment of individual works organized my motif; the second dealing with structure, style, substance, scientific content, and bias. The last three chapters of this section are organized by theme or motif. An extensive and still useful bibliography is included.

125. Blish, James (as William Atheling, Jr.). *The Issue at Hand: Studies in Contemporary Magazine Science Fiction.* Chicago: Advent, 1964. 136pp.

A collection of reviews and critical commentary written between 1952 and 1963 on American magazine science fiction of the time. The material consists of short essays that Blish contributed to fan magazines, and two World Science Fiction Convention speeches.

126. Blish, James (as William Atheling, Jr.). *More Issues at Hand: Critical Studies in Contemporary Science Fiction.* Chicago: Advent, 1970. 154pp.

Continuing his critical commentaries on science fiction, Blish turns to the books written between

1957 and 1970, concluding with a look at the "New
Wave." The essays consist of material that appeared
in various fan magazines, and in *Science Fiction
Times; Magazine of Fantasy & Science Fiction; Science Fiction Forum;* and *SF Horizons.*

127. Bova, Ben[jamin]. *Notes to a Science Fiction Writer.*
     New York: Charles Scribner's Sons, 1975. 177pp.

The editor of *Analog* offers basic advice on the
craft of writing science fiction. The book deals
with short story writing only, and focuses on four
areas of study--character, background, conflict,
and plot--with a wrap-up section on manuscript preparation, cover letters, and other miscellaneous
items. A practical manual that nicely complements
L. Sprague de Camp's more general work, *The Science
Fiction Handbook, Revised* (which see).

128. Bretnor, Reginald, ed. *The Craft of Science Fiction.*
     New York: Harper & Row, 1976. 321pp.

The primary purpose of this book is to remind the
writer that "writing good sf demands much knowledge
and many new perspectives not essential to what is
generally called 'mainstream' fiction"; the writer
must "avoid the still too prevalent delusion that
science really has little or nothing to do with
science fiction." The essays deal with how SF is
written rather than with how to write SF and will
appeal to anyone wishing to explore the imaginative
richness of science fiction via the particular per-
ceptions of some of the field's leading practitioners.

129. **Bretnor**, Reginald, ed. *Modern Science Fiction: Its
     Meaning and Its Future.* New York: Coward-McCann,
     1953. 294pp.

One of the earliest comprehensive symposiums on
modern science fiction (preceded by *Of Worlds Beyond,* a shorter essay collection edited by Lloyd
Eshbach published in 1947). While partially dated,
the eleven essays by writers, critics, and editors
comprise an important document of SF's Golden Age.
Contents comprise: "The Place of Science Fiction"
by John W. Campbell, Jr., "The Publishing of Science
Fiction" by Anthony Boucher, "Science Fiction in
the Motion Pictures, Radio, and Television" by Don
Fabun, "A Critique of Science Fiction" by Fletcher
Pratt, "Science Fiction and the Main Stream" by
Rosalie Moore, "Imaginative Fiction and Creative
Imagination" by L. Sprague de Camp, "Social Science
Fiction" by Isaac Asimov, "Science Fiction: Prepar-
ation for the Age of Space" by Arthur C. Clarke,

"Science Fiction and Sanity in an Age of Crisis" by
Philip Wylie, "Science Fiction, Morals, and Religion"
by Gerald Heard, and "The Future of Science Fiction"
by Reginald Bretnor.

130. Bretnor, Reginald, ed. *Science Fiction, Today and
     Tomorrow*. New York: Harper & Row, 1974. 342pp.

An anthology of essays by SF writers about the nature
of their genre, art, and craft. Contents: "The Role
of Science Fiction" by Ben Bova, "The Publishing of
Science Fiction" by Frederik Pohl, "Science Fiction
and the Visual Media" by George Zebrowski, "Science
Fiction and a World in Crisis" by Frank Herbert,
"Science Fiction, Morals, and Religion" by Theodore
Sturgeon, "Science Fiction and Man's Adaptation to
Change" by Alan E. Nourse, "Science Fiction as the
Imaginary Experiment" by Thomas N. Scortia, "Science
Fiction in the Age of Space" by Reginald Bretnor,
"Science Fiction and the Mainstream" by James Gunn,
"Science Fiction, New Trends and Old" by Alexei and
Cory Panshin, "The Creation of Imaginary Worlds" by
Poul Anderson, "The Creation of Imaginary Beings"
by Hal Clement, "Romance and Glamour in Science
Fiction" by Anne McCaffrey, "Plausibility in Science
Fiction" by Gordon R. Dickson, "Science Fiction,
Teaching, and Criticism" by Jack Williamson, and
"A Critical Sampler."

131. Carter, Lin. *Imaginary Worlds: The Art of Fantasy*.
     New York: Ballantine Books, 1973. 278pp. [paper].

A historical survey of modern heroic fantasy from
William Morris to the present. Includes coverage of
major genre authors (Morris, Dunsany, Eddison, Cabell, Hodgson, Howard, Lovecraft, C.S. Lewis, and
Tolkien) and analyzes their contribution to and influence on the genre. Some chapters are organized
around a specific group, magazine influence, or sub-
genre, e.g., the Inklings, the Munsey magazines,
Weird Tales, Unknown, Sword & Sorcery   Includes
three chapters on the technique of writing fantasy.

132. Cawelti, John G. *Adventure, Mystery and Romance:
     Formula Stories as Art and Popular Culture*.
     Chicago and London: University of Chicago Press,
     1976. 336pp.

A study of the popular story formulas. The author
deals "intensively with a few major formulas--var-
ious forms of detective and crime stories, the
western, and the best-selling social melodrama."
A useful work for students of popular culture and
of the pulp magazine period in the popular arts.

133. Chauvin, Cy, ed. *A Multitude of Visions: Essays on Science Fiction*. Baltimore: T-K Graphics, 1975. 67pp. [paper].

Eight critical essays on science fiction authors and themes selected from *Scythrop, Quicksilver, Quarber Merkur*, and other fanzines. Contents: "The View In" by Ursula K. Le Guin, "Representation in SF" by Thomas M. Disch, "Vector Zero: The SF Story in the Seventies" by Bruce R. Gillespie, "'After Such Knowledge': James Blish's Tetralogy" by Bob Rickard, "Science and Reality in Philip K. Dick's 'Ubik'" by Stanislaw Lem, "'Arrive at Easterwine': Some Arrant Roadmapping" by Sheryl Smith, "'Franken-stein Unbound': The Regeneration of a Myth" by Jeff Clark, and "The Arts in Science Fiction" by James Blish.

134. Clareson, Thomas D. *SF: A Dream of Other Worlds*. College Station, TX: Texas A&M University Library, 1973. 15pp. [paper].

A lecture on the origins of modern science fiction, based in part on Dr. Clareson's introductory essay to his anthology *A Spectrum of Worlds* (Doubleday, 1972).

135. Clareson, Thomas D., ed. *Many Futures, Many Worlds: Theme and Form in Science Fiction*. [Kent, OH]: Kent State University Press, 1977. 303pp.

A collection of essays approaching the study of science fiction from starting points as diverse as philosophy, mythology, theology, and technology as well as touching upon such established themes as time travel, lost races, and computerized govern-ments. Contents: "Perception and Value in Science Fiction" by Thomas L. Wymer, "Many Futures, Many Worlds" by Thomas D. Clareson, "The Science in Science Fiction" by Stanley Schmidt, "Revivals of Ancient Mythologies in Current Science Fiction and Fantasy" by S.C. Fredericks, "Tyranny by Computer: Automated Data Processing and Oppressive Government in Science Fiction" by Carolyn C. Rhodes, "The Known and the Unknown: Structure and Image in Sci-ence Fiction" by Gary K. Wolfe, "Lost Lands, Lost Races: A Pagan Princess of Their Very Own" by Thomas D. Clareson, "Virgin Territory: The Bonds and Bound-aries of Women in Science Fiction" by Beverly Friend, "Science Fiction as Fictive History" by Robert H. Canary, "Images of the Man-Machine Intelligence Re-lationship in Science Fiction" by Patricia Warrick, "Science Fiction as Simulation Game" by Steven Kagle,

"Theology, Science Fiction, and Man's Future Orientation" by J. Norman King, "The Philosophical Limitations of Science Fiction" by Patrick G. Hogan, Jr., and "Critical Methods: Speculative Fiction" by Samuel R. Delany.

136. Clareson, Thomas D., ed. *SF: The Other Side of Realism: Essays on Modern Fantasy and Science Fiction.* Bowling Green, OH: Bowling Green University Popular Press, 1971. 356pp.

From a multitude of critical viewpoints the contributors to this pioneer anthology illustrate the many ways in which the study of science fiction may be approached. Contents: "The Other Side of Realism" by Thomas D. Clareson, "Realism and Fantasy" by Julius Kagarlitski, "What Do You Mean: Science? Fiction?" by Judith Merril, "The Artistic Problem: Science Fiction as Romance" by Lionel Stevenson, "Fantasy as Technique" by Rudolf B. Schmerl, "The Wounded Land: J.G. Ballard" by Brian Aldiss, "About Five Thousand One Hundred and Seventy-Five Words" by Samuel R. Delany, "The Two Gardens in C.S. Lewis's *That Hideous Strength*" by Patrick J. Callahan, "Science Fiction: The Crisis of Its Growth" by Michel Butor, "On Science Fiction Criticism" by James Blish, "*Frankenstein,* Mary Shelley's Black Theodicy" by Milton A. Mays, "*Stand on Zanzibar:* The Novel as Film" by Norman Spinrad, "*The Last* And First *Starship From Earth*" by Jane Hipolito, "Science Fiction the Modern Mythology [Vonnegut's *Slaughterhouse-Five*]" by Willis E. McNelly, "Forword to J.G. Ballard's 'The Subliminal Man'" by Bruce Franklin, "The Publication of *The Time Machine,* 1894-1895" by Bernard Bergonzi, "The Shape of Wars to Come" by I.F. Clarke, "The Undisciplined Imagination: Edgar Rice Burroughs and Lowellian Mars" by Richard D. Mullen, "A Short Tragical History of the Science Fiction Film" by Richard Hodgens, "Three Perspectives of a Film" by Morris Beja, Robert Plank and Alex Eisenstein, "Science Fiction as a Cultural Phenomenon: A Re-Evaluation" by Mark R. Hillegas, "A Poetic Precursor to Bellamy's *Looking Backward*" by Ben Fuson, "Kurd Lasswitz: A German Pioneer of Science Fiction" by Franz Rottensteiner, "Robots in Science Fiction" by Stanislaw Lem, "Science Fiction in Dimension" by Alexie Panshin, "'A City of Which the Stars are Suburbs'" by Susan Glicksohn, and "Award-Winning Science Fiction Novels."

137. Davenport, Basil. *Inquiry Into Science Fiction*.
New York: Longmans, Green, 1955. 87pp.

A brief but cogent discussion of the history,
method, and "mystique" of science fiction. Topics
covered include space opera, scientific SF, the
emotional impact of SF, and the future of the genre.
Important as a historical document.

138. Davenport, Basil, [ed.] *The Science Fiction Novel:
Imagination and Social Criticism*. Chicago:
Advent, 1959. 128pp.

The text of four lectures by Robert A. Heinlein,
C.M. Kornbluth, Alfred Bester, and Robert Bloch
delivered at the University of Chicago in 1957
which are critical of the role of science fiction
as social criticism. Introduction by Basil Davenport. Useful for historical perspective.

139. De Camp, L. Sprague. *Literary Swordsmen and Sorcerers: The Makers of Heroic Fantasy*. Sauk City, WI:
Arkham House, 1976. 313pp.

The evolution of Sword & Sorcery fantasy through
biographical sketches of its leading practitioners
whose works were central to the growth of the genre.
Authors treated are William Morris, Lord Dunsany,
H.P. Lovecraft, E.R. Eddison, Robert E. Howard,
Fletcher Pratt, Clark Ashton Smith, J.R.R. Tolkien,
and T.H. White. Most of the chapters are expanded
versions of articles that appeared in *Arma* and *Fantastic Stories*; the Howard chapter has also been
published as *The Miscast Barbarian* (Gerry de la Ree,
1975). A major contribution to the study of heroic
fantasy.

140. De Camp, L. Sprague. *Science-Fiction Handbook: The
Writing of Imaginative Fiction*. New York: Hermi-
tage House, 1953. 328pp. Rev. ed. *Science Fiction
Handbook, Revised*. Philadelphia: Owlswick Press,
1975. 220pp. Revision in collaboration with
Catherine Crook de Camp.

The 1953 edition of the *Handbook* is a historic document which analyzes the state of the art and the
market at the height of the Golden Age of SF. The
1975 revision exhibits a number of alterations. While
the trade information has been updated and a chapter,
"The Business Side of Writing," has been added, the
remainder of the text has been considerably condensed.
The excellent short survey of imaginative fiction
which comprised 81 pages in the original edition
has been trimmed to 50. The revised version also

38

deletes a chapter, "Writers of Imaginative Fiction,"
containing informative biographies of eighteen representative SF writers active in the 1950s "who have
made the most money from writing imaginative fiction." Students of science fiction history should
refer to the earlier edition.

141. Delany, Samuel R. *The Jewel-Hinged Jaw: Notes on
the Language of Science Fiction.* Elizabethtown,
NY: Dragon Press, 1977. 326pp.

A collection of critical essays on science fiction
critical theory, writing SF, and author studies.
This latter section includes studies of Thomas M.
Disch and Roger Zelazny, Joanna Russ, Disch again
(an analysis of the structure of the dream scene in
Camp Concentration), and the book's major essay, an
extended study of Ursula K. Le Guin's *The Dispossessed*). The first of two volumes of criticism by Delany
to be issued by Dragon Press. Volume Two, *The American Shore* [in press at this time], is a book-length
study of Thomas M. Disch's story, "Angouleme," which
forms part of a sequence of *334*.

142. Eshbach, Lloyd Arthur, ed. *Of Worlds Beyond: The
Science of Science Fiction Writing.* Reading, PA:
Fantasy Press, 1947. 96pp. Rpt. Chicago: Advent,
1964. 104pp. Index added to this edition.

The first anthology of essays on writing science
fiction by seven of the field's leading practitioners. Contents: "On the Writing of Speculative Fiction" by Robert A. Heinlein, "Writing a Science
Novel" by John Taine, "The Logic of Fantasy" by Jack
Williamson, "Complication in the Science Fiction
Story" by A.E. Van Vogt, "Humor in Science Fiction"
by L. Sprague de Camp, "The Epic of Space" by Edward
E. Smith, and "The Science of Science Fiction Writing" by John W. Campbell, Jr.

143. Franklin, H. Bruce, ed. *Future Perfect: American
Science Fiction of the Nineteenth Century.* New
York: Oxford University Press, 1966. 402pp.

An anthology of 19th century American science fiction with extensive critical commentary by the
editor which remains the most perceptive and pro-
vocative study of science fiction by American literary figures of the period.

144. Frye, Northrop. *The Secular Scripture: A Study of
the Structure of Romance.* Cambridge, MA: Harvard
University Press, 1976. 199pp.

The texts of the Charles Eliot Norton Lectures,
1974-1975 at Harvard. Frye contends that the structure of the Bible provided the outline for the basic
conventions of Romance. A discussion of the conventions of Romance as established in the late Classical
period, tracing them to such modern genres as the
detective story and science fiction.

145. Gunn, James. *Alternate Worlds: The Illustrated His-
tory of Science Fiction.* Englewood Cliffs, NJ:
Prentice-Hall, 1975. 256pp. Rpt. New York: A&W
Visual Library, 1976. [paper].

Gunn, an award-winning science fiction author and
respected literary scholar, here provides an inform-
ed study of the scientific, social and philosophical
climate which brought forth and shaped science fiction from its early beginnings to the present. Gunn
devoted many years to gathering the illustrations,
which include many rare photographs of SF writers,
editors, critics, and fans, which compliment the
highly readable text. Certainly the most ambitious
of the published histories of science fiction to
date. Well indexed.

146. Gunn, James. *The Discovery of the Future: The Ways
Science Fiction Developed.* College Station, TX:
Texas A&M University Library, 1975. 17pp. [paper].

A general statement on the emergence of science fiction from the literary mainstream during the Indus-
trial Revolution and its current status, delivered
as a lecture at the dedication of the Science Fiction
Research Collection of Texas A&M University in 1974.

147. Hillegas, Mark R. *The Future as Nightmare.* (See
III B2)

148. Irwin, W.R. *The Game of the Impossible: A Rhetoric
of Fantasy.* Urbana: University of Illinois Press,
1976. 215pp.

An examination of the common characteristics of fantasies written between 1880 and 1957. Establishes
that "a fantasy is a story based on and controlled
by an overt violation of what is generally accepted
as possibility." Selected works by C.S. Lewis,
Franz Kafka, Ronald Firbank, David Garnett, Herbert
Read, Elinor Wylie, W.H. Hudson, Virginia Woolf,
J.R.R. Tolkien and others are analyzed for their
intrinsic importance and illustrative value. Contains
a selected annotated bibliography of fantasy fiction.

149. Ketterer, David. *New Worlds for Old: The Apocalyptic Imagination, Science Fiction, and American Literature.* Bloomington and London: Indiana University Press, 1974. 347pp.

An attempt to place the literature of science fiction within the broader category of the "apocalyptic"-- literature that concerns itself with the "destruction of an old world and the coming of a new order." Ketterer maintains that "because of a common apocalyptic quality and a common grounding in the romance, science fiction and mainstream American literature share many significant features." An important scholarly study and the first book-length treatment of science fiction to give sustained explication of contemporary texts. One of its twelve chapters is devoted to Ursula Le Guin.

150. Knight, Damon. *In Search of Wonder: Essays on Modern Science Fiction.* Chicago: Advent, 1956. 180pp. Rev. ed. Chicago: Advent, 1967. 306pp.

A collection of critical book reviews written by Knight for the *Magazine of Fantasy & Science Fiction* from 1952 to 1955. The revised edition adds reviews written from 1956-1960, along with some new material. The book consists of a disconnected series of brief comments on some of the science fiction of the period, but lacking an underlying theme. The reviews, however, are in themselves witty, intelligent, and perceptive, if occasionally biased.

151. Knight, Damon, ed. *Turning Points: Essays on the Art of Science Fiction.* New York: Harper & Row, 1977. 303pp.

Collects twenty-three essays on science fiction culled from diverse sources spanning nearly three decades of critical statements on the genre. Contents: "Science Fiction: Its Nature, Faults and Virtues" by Robert A. Heinlein, "Social Science Fiction" by Isaac Asimov, "What Is Science Fiction?" by Damon Knight, "Pilgrim Fathers: Lucian and All That" by Brian W. Aldiss, "Science Fiction Before Gernsback" by H. Bruce Franklin, "The Situation Today" by Kingsley Amis, "On Science Fiction" by C.S. Lewis, "Alien Monsters" by Joanna Russ, "Cathedrals in Space" by James Blish, "Contact" by Pierre Versins, "No Copying Allowed" by John W. Campbell, "Scientists in S.F.: A Debate" by Philip R. Geffe, Milton R. Rothman, John W. Campbell, James V. McConnell, "On the Writing of Speculative Fiction" by Robert A. Heinlein, "How to Build a Planet" by Poul Anderson, "How to

Collaborate Without Getting Your Head Shaved" by
Keith Laumer, "Writing and Selling Science Fiction"
by Damon Knight, "Chemical Persuasion" by Aldous
Huxley, "Pandora's Box" by Robert A. Heinlein, "Gour-
met Dining in Outer Space" by Alfred Bester, "Why
So Much Syzygy?" by Theodore Sturgeon, "There's
Nothing Like a Good Foundation" by Asaac Asimov,
"Son of Dr. Strangelove" by Arthur C. Clarke, "Jour-
ney with a Little Man" by Richard McKenna.

152. Kyle, David. *A Pictorial History of Science Fiction*.
London: Hamlyn, 1976. 173pp.

Lacks the scope of Gunn's *Alternate Worlds* (which
see) but is still one of the best illustrated his-
tories of science fiction. Comparable in scope to
Franz Rottensteiner, *The Science Fiction Book: An
Illustrated History* (London: Thames and Hudson,
1975), with the exception of the coverage of non-
English works, for which the latter is especially
valuable (the English language editions of Rottensteiner have a number of translator's errors).
Jacques Sadoul, *2000 A.D.: Illustrations from the
Golden Age of Science Fiction Pulps* (Chicago: Henry
Regnery, 1975) reproduces illustrations from the
1926-1953 period and is more pictorial than Rottensteiner, but lacks its historical and critical scope.
Anthony Frewin, *One Hundred Years of Science Fiction
Illustration, 1840-1940* (London: Jupiter Books, 1974)
is of value for its emphasis on 19th century fantasy
illustrations (covering the work of Grandville, Ro-
bida, and illustrations from books by Verne and
Wells as well as turn-of-the-century British and
American popular magazines). The illustrations are
well captioned and while the remaining text is brief,
it is helpful in relating SF art to the fiction it
depicted. Brian W. Aldiss, *Science Fiction Art* (London: New English Library, 1975) is probably the best
study of SF art to date. This large format book provides a good general survey with an excellent introduction, an artist's showcase which presents a fine
sampling of the work of thirty American and British
illustrators, thematic sections, and a magazine gal-
lery reproducing covers of 79 representative SF
titles. Lester del Rey, ed., *Fantastic Science Fiction Art, 1926-1954* (New York: Ballantine Books,
1975) provides a good general essay on the subject
and reproduces 40 magazine covers with too much emphasis on the work of Frank R. Paul.

153. Lovecraft, Howard Phillips. *Supernatural Horror in
Literature*. New York: Ben Abramson, 1945. 111pp.
Rpt. New York: Dover Publications, 1973. [paper].

A critical survey of the history of horror fiction
by the most important American supernaturalist since
Poe. Originally published in *The Recluse* in 1927, it
was later revised and serialized in *The Fantasy Fan*.
Editors August Derleth and Donald Wandrei established
the final text for the Lovecraft memorial volume,
The Outsider and Others, published in 1939 by Arkham
House. The Dover edition contains a new introduction
by E.F. Bleiler.

154. Lowndes, Robert A.W. *Three Faces of Science Fiction*.
     Boston: NESFA Press, 1973. 96pp.

An informal discussion of science fiction as in-
struction, as propaganda, and as delight (this
latter section concentrates on the work of Verne,
Wells, Burroughs, E.E. Smith, Heinlein, and Blish),
being a revision of a series of editorials appearing
during 1967-68 in *Famous Science Fiction*. Lowndes,
a noted SF editor, was literary director of the entire chain of Columbia pulps from 1942 to 1960 and
from 1956 through 1967 edited a series of 136 SF
titles for Avalon books.

155. Lundwall, Sam J. *Science Fiction: What It's All
     About*. New York: Ace Books, 1971. 256pp. [paper].

An informal historical survey of science fiction
aimed at the popular market. Relies on popular
secondary sources for the history of the genre.
Of interest for commentary on heroic fantasy, SF
as popular culture, and fan activity.

156. Moskowitz, Sam. *Explorers of the Infinite: Shapers
     of Science Fiction*. Cleveland and New York:
     World Publishing, 1963. 353pp. Rpt. Westport,
     CT: Hyperion Press, 1974.

Moskowitz's historical approach to the study of science fiction is firmly rooted in the Gernsback tra-
dition--a sense of wonder anchored in verisimilitude
as exemplified by Poe and Verne. In general this
work suffers from a lack of critical insight and a
failure to relate the SF genre to wider literary
or historical traditions. In spite of these defi-
ciences, his indefatigable historical researches
into pre-World War II science fiction deserves
careful study. Moskowitz has outlined previously
uncharted regions of the SF tradition, especially
those contributions to English and American popular
magazines of the late Victorian and Edwardian eras
and the pre-Gernsback American pulp magazines.
Explorers emphasizes pre-Gernsback writers who influenced the developing genre--Cyrano de Bergerac,

Shelley, Poe, Verne, Wells, Arthur Conan Doyle,
Burroughs, Stapledon. Of special interest are
chapters on Fitz-James O'Brien, M.P. Shiel, A.
Merritt, Karel Capek, H.P. Lovecraft, Philip Wylie,
and Stanley G. Weinbaum.

157. Moskowitz, Sam. *The Immortal Storm: A History of
Science-Fiction Fandom*. Atlanta: Burwell, 1951.
Rpt. Atlanta: Atlanta Science Fiction Organiza-
tion Press, 1954. 269pp. Rpt. Westport, CT:
Hyperion Press, 1974.

A personal view of fandom, but still the best picture of this small but influential group of SF
activists. Much historical data on the fanzines of
the 1930s and 1940s unavailable elsewhere.

158. Moskowitz, Sam. *Seekers of Tomorrow: Masters of
Modern Science Fiction*. Cleveland and New York:
World Publishing, 1966. 441pp. Rpt. Westport, CT:
Hyperion Press, 1974.

A companion volume to *Explorers of the Infinite*
which sketches the biography and works of twenty-
one modern science fiction authors from "bridge
authors"--E.E. Smith, John W. Campbell, Murray Leinster and Edmond Hamilton--to Wyndham, Russell, de
Camp, Del Rey, Heinlein, Van Vogt, Sturgeon, Asimov,
Simak, Leiber, Moore, Kuttner, Bloch, Bradbury,
Clarke and Farmer.

159. Moskowitz, Sam. *Strange Horizons: The Spectrum of
Science Fiction*. New York: Charles Scribner's
Sons, 1976. 298pp.

This attempt to trace sociological themes in science
fiction suffers from a lack of critical and historical viewpoint which does much to damage his observations and conclusions. For example, his chapter
"Civil Rights" examines the depiction of Blacks in
science fiction, but omitted from consideration are
a number of novels and stories including two significant early treatments: Shirley T. Hodge's *The
White Man's Burden* (1915), which depicts noble and
compassionate Blacks in control of a worldwide utopia; and King Wallace's *The Next War* (1892), which
concerns a Black plot to destroy the White race.
The limits of Moskowitz's reading of little known
early works and, more important, post-World War II
authors, are evident in this volume. Other themes
surveyed include women's liberation, birth control,
crime, teenagers, war, art, and religion.

160. Mullen, R.D. and Darko Suvin, eds. *Science-Fiction Studies: Selected Articles on Science Fiction 1973-1975*. Boston: Gregg Press, 1976. 304pp.

Fifty essays selected from *Science-Fiction Studies*, one of the major international scholarly journals devoted to the serious study of science fiction. In six sections the anthology covers science fiction and literary theory, social criticism in science fiction, 19th century science fiction, history of science fiction, and critical appraisals of several modern writers, with special attention to Ursula K. Le Guin and Philip K. Dick. Includes essays by Brian Aldiss, James Blish, Philip K. Dick, Damon Knight, H. Bruce Franklin, Stanislaw Lem, Ursula K. Le Guin, Robert Philmus, Franz Rottensteiner, Joanna Russ, Robert Scholes, Darko Suvin, and others.

161. Nicholls, Peter, ed. *Science Fiction at Large: A Collection of Essays, by Various Hands, About the Interface Between Science Fiction and Reality*. London: Gollancz, 1976. 224pp. Rpt. New York: Harper & Row, 1977.

A collection of lectures delivered at the Institute of Contemporary Arts in London, 1975. Aimed at the general science fiction readership. Contents: "Science Fiction and Mrs Brown" by Ursula K. Le Guin, "Lateral Thinking and Science Fiction" by Edward De Bono, "Scientific Thought in Fiction and in Fact" by John Taylor, "Science Fiction and the Larger Lunacy" by John Brunner, "Worlds Beside Worlds" by Harry Harrison, "Science Fiction and Change" by Alan Toffler, "Inner Time" by Alan Garner, "The Embarrassments of Science Fiction" by Thomas M. Disch, "Science Fiction: The Monsters and the Critics" by Peter Nicholls, "The Search for the Marvellous" by Robert Sheckley, and "Man, Android and Machine" by Philip K. Dick.

162. Panshin, Alexei and Cory. *SF in Dimension: A Book of Explorations*. Chicago: Advent, 1976. 342pp.

Based on a series of essays written by Alexei for *Fantastic Stories*, in which he attempts to "redefine the nature of science fiction as a literary form."

163. Penzoldt, Peter. *The Supernatural in Fiction*. London: Peter Nevill, 1952. 271pp. Rpt. New York: Humanities Press, 1965.

A study of the English short story of the supernatural divided into two parts: the first, a survey
of the entire field which treats the origin, structure and major motifs of the weird tale; the second,
a detailed analysis of the works of Le Fanu, Dickens,
Stevenson, Kipling, M.R. James, de la Mare, and
Blackwood, with sub-chapters on F.M. Crawford,
Machen, Lovecraft, L.P. Hartley, Henry James, and
Wells. Science fiction is inadequately dealt with
in a brief section headed "The Supernatural in
Science Fiction."

164. Philmus, Robert M. *Into the Unknown: The Evolution
of Science Fiction from Francis Godwin to H.G.
Wells.* Berkeley: University of California Press,
1970. 174pp.

A survey of English science fiction of the 18th and
19th centuries in which the author explains science
fiction as "a rhetorical technique which uses plaus-
ible scientific explanations to cause the reader to
suspend his disbelief and accept fantastic situa-
tions." Philmus further relates science fiction to
utopian satire and to a mythological view of life.

165. [Porter, Andrew, ed.] *Experiment Perilous: Three
Essays on Science Fiction.* New York: Algol Press,
1976. 34pp. [paper].

Contains "Experiment Perilous: The Art and Science
of Anguish in Science Fiction" by Marion Zimmer
Bradley (*Algol,* November 1972), "The Bug Jack Barron Papers" by Norman Spinrad (*Algol,* Spring 1969),
and "Writing and *The Demolished Man*" by Alfred Bester (*Algol,* May 1972).

166. Rabkin, Eric S. *The Fantastic in Literature.*
Princeton: Princeton University Press, 1976.
234pp.

An exploration of the nature and uses of the fantastic following from the recognition that it is not
the unreal which is fantastic but the unreal in a
particular context. Each chapter develops this view,
using examples from fairy tales, detective fiction,
science fiction, utopian fiction, the Gothic, and
traditional literature. A theoretical introduction
to an increasingly popular mode of narrative.

167. Rose, Mark, ed. *Science Fiction: A Collection of
Critical Essays.* Englewood Cliffs, NJ: Prentice-
Hall, 1976. 169pp.

Eleven essays reprinted from various scholarly and
academic sources grouped under the headings: backgrounds, theory, and approaches. Many of the essays
are highly theoretical and will be of interest only
to those readers with more than a passing interest
in the genre. Contents: "Staring Points" by Kingsley Amis, "Science Fiction and Literature" by Robert
Conquest, "The Roots of Science Fiction" by Robert
Scholes, "On the Poetics of the Science Fiction
Genre" by Darko Suvin, "The Time-Travel Story and
Related Matters" by Stanislaw Lem, "Genre Criticism"
by Eric S. Rabkin, "On Science Fiction" by C.S.
Lewis, "The Imagination of Disaster" by Susan Son-
tag, "How to Play Utopia: Some Brief Notes on the
Distinctiveness of Utopian Fiction" by Michael
Holquist, "The Apocalyptic Imagination, Science
Fiction, and American Literature" by David Ketterer,
and "Science Fiction and the Future" by John Hunt-
ington.

168. Samuelson, David. *Visions of Tomorrow*. (See IV A)

169. Scholes, Robert. *Structural Fabulation: An Essay on
     the Fiction of the Future*. Notre Dame: University
     of Notre Dame Press, 1975. 111pp.

Based on four lectures deliverd at the University
of Notre Dame in 1974, this critical and theoretical
study of science fiction relates the genre to the
literary traditions and to modern intellectual history, arguing for the seriousness of science fiction
and its value as literature. Devotes an entire chapter to Ursula K. Le Guin. An important book that may
have an influence in the field similar to that of
Kingsley Amis' *New Maps of Hell* (which see).

170. Scholes, Robert and Eric S. Rabkin. *Science Fiction:
     History, Science, Vision*. New York: Oxford Uni-
     versity Press, 1977. 258pp.

This textbook survey of science fiction offers a
synthesis of the historical, scientific, and thematic
elements that comprise the genre. The book is divided
into three distinct but interrelated sections: "History," a lengthy summary of literary developments
and major writers; "Science," a brief history of the
evolution of scientific ideas and their impact on
literature; and "Vision," a discussion of the forms,
themes, and social concerns of science fiction, with
critical readings of ten novels: *Frankenstein, 20,000
Leagues Under the Sea, The Time Machine, We, A Voyage
to Arcturus, Star Maker, Childhood's End, A Canticle
for Leibowitz, The Left Hand of Darkness,* and *The
Shockwave Rider.*

171. Smith, Clark Ashton. *Planets and Dimensions: Collected Essays*. Ed. Charles K. Wolfe. Baltimore: Mirage Press, 1973. 87pp.

Collects most of Smith's important non-fiction, comprising essays, book reviews, and letters published in the professional and amateur magazines from 1937 through 1953, with the most frequent topic being his own theories about weird and speculative fiction, as well as homage to those who influenced his art: George Sterling, H.P. Lovecraft, M.R. James, Ambrose Bierce, Poe, and others. Editor Wolfe notes that Smith's critical statements "provide one of the most cogent and well-informed aesthetics evolved and articulated by any major writer of speculative fiction."

172. Todorov, Tzvetan. *The Fantastic: A Structural Approach to a Literary Genre*. Tr. Richard Howard. Cleveland and London: The Press of Case Western Reserve University, 1973. 179pp.

This study is "not simply another 'formalist' categorizing of a particular literary genre. Todorov involves himself in a consideration of the concept of a literary genre, . . . a detailed and perceptive discourse on 'the fantastic' (relating it to, and distinguishing it from, 'the uncanny,' 'the marvelous,' 'allegory,' and other genres or sub-genres of fiction), and finally a philosophical-historical discussion of the relation of 'the fantastic' to literature itself."

173. Warner, Harry, Jr. *All Our Yesterdays: An Informal History of Science Fiction Fandom in the Forties*. Chicago: Advent, 1969. 336pp.

This work, despite its intentional lack of critical apparatus, is still of value for its numerous biographical sketches of prominent fans (including those who became professional SF writers and editors) and commentary upon fan activities (clubs, conventions, amateur press associations, publications, controversies). More informal than Moskowitz's *The Immortal Storm* (which see), it is nonetheless the more balanced and impersonal statement. The fragmented arrangement of material is offset by extensive indexing.

174. Wilson, Colin. *The Strength to Dream: Literature and the Imagination*. Boston: Houghton Mifflin, 1962. 277pp. Rpt. Westport, CT: GReenwood Press, 1973.

A discussion of the role of the imagination in modern literature and its relation to values in writers.

Includes major discussions of H.P. Lovecraft, H.G.
Wells, Zamiatin, Le Fanu and M.R. James, Tolkien,
and briefly notes the following science fictional
topics: utopias and anti-utopias, science fiction
and space opera, popular science fiction, and ghosts
and the supernatural.

175. Wollheim, Donald A. *The Universe Makers: Science
Fiction Today*. New York: Harper & Row, 1971.
122pp.

A personal statement of the place of science fiction in literature via discussions of the most important writers of the genre. Establishes Verne and
Wells as the two traditions and divides SF into
four major classifications: imaginary voyages, future predictions, remarkable inventions, and social
satire. An excellent introduction to the genre for
the beginning student of science fiction.

(4) Magazine Surveys & Histories

a. General

176. Ashley, Michael, ed. *The History of the Science
Fiction Magazine*. 3 vols. London: New English
Library, 1974-76. 239, 298, 349pp. Rpt. Chicago:
Henry Regnery, 1976.

The first three volumes of a projected five volume
series, each examining a decade of the SF magazine
from 1926 to 1976. More an anthology of science
fiction than a history, each volume features ten
selections from the magazines, prefaced by historical commentary by the editor. The introductions
lack critical insight and are informal in tone, but
they provide a balanced compact historical overview
of the SF magazine, and are especially valuable for
data on British publications. Appendices for each
volume include a checklist of fiction by authors
represented in the collection (in volumes one and
three there are checklists for ten and eleven additional authors respectively), a summary of magazine
issues, a listing of editors and the magazine issues for which they were responsible, and a listing
of cover artists.

177. Goulart, Ron. *An Informal History of the Pulp
Magazines*. New York: Ace Books, 1972. 192pp.
[paper].

A lively survey of the rise and fall of the pulp
era, beginning with Frank Munsey's publication of
the first number of the *Golden Argosy* in 1882. Chapters on Doc Savage, Edgar Rice Burroughs, Robert E.
Howard, and the SF pulps.

178. Jones, Robert Kenneth. *The Shudder Pulps: A History
of the Weird Menace Magazines of the 1930's*.
West Linn, OR: FAX Collector's Editions, 1975.
238pp.

The weird menace sub-genre emerged from the detective
pulps in the October 1933 issue of *Dime Detective*.
A unique combination of sadism, gothic terror, and
a rational resolution of a seemingly supernatural
manifestation comprised the basic formula for these
specialty pulps, which often employed a weird menace
plot with a science fiction theme. After a peak in
the late thirties, the combination of plot formula
alterations, rising costs, competition with the
comic market, and World War II accompanied by a new
public morality, brought an end to this type of pulp
in 1941. The present volume is not a study of the
social significance of these pulps, nor does it relate them to the wider literary or historical tradition. Jones presents a history of the magazines,
their publishers, editors, and writers and discusses
their literary characteristics, including themes,
plots, and writing styles. The work is indexed, but
regretably contains no checklist of magazines and
publishing data, thus somewhat limiting the overall
value of the work. Of interest to the specialist.

179. Jones, Robert Kenneth. *The Weird Menace*. (See
III B4a)

180. Moskowitz, Sam, ed. *Science Fiction by Gaslight: A
History and Anthology of Science Fiction in the
Popular Magazines, 1891-1911*. Cleveland: World
Publishing, 1968. 364pp. Rpt. New York: Hyperion
Press, 1974.

An anthology of twenty-six selections from American
and British periodicals arranged by motif. The
thirty-six page introduction is one of Moskowitz's
most important contributions to the study of science
fiction history. He charts the early history of the
mass-circulation, general interest English language
magazine and, through his historical survey and representative fiction selection, examines the themes
and extent of a popular literary form of the period.

181. Moskowitz, Sam, ed. *Under the Moons of Mars: A History and Anthology of "The Scientific Romance" in the Munsey Magazines, 1912-1920.* New York: Holt, Rinehart & Winston, 1970. 433pp.

In part, a continuation of the examination of science fiction in popular magazines begun in *Science Fiction by Gaslight,* though here the study is restricted to American periodicals with emphasis on the Munsey group. In this valuable 143-page historical survey Moskowitz traces the influence of Edgar Rice Burroughs, whose scientific romances sacrificed verisimilitude for romantic adventure. The scientific romance was a dominant literary form during this transitional period and the popular fiction magazine was the major vehicle for this type of fiction. Inadequate references and the lack of index and bibliography limit the usefulness of this study.

182. Wertham, Fredric. *The World of Fanzines: A Special Form of Communication.* Carbondale: Southern Illinois University Press, 1973. 144pp.

The focus of this book is descriptive and analytical. Wertham examines the fanzines' content (art and text), circulation, and methods of production, and analyzes their influence as a manifestation of creativity--as something apart from "little magazines" and underground newspapers.

b. Individual

183. Eisgruber, Frank, Jr. *Gangland's Doom: The Shadow of the Pulps.* Oak Lawn, IL: Robert Weinberg, 1974. 64pp. [paper].

An informal assemblage of data on *The Shadow Magazine* (1931-1949). Neither a history nor an analysis of the pulp, this work provides details on the fictional characters--the Shadow and his various guises, his allies and enemies--and story settings. Included is a list of the 325 novels featuring this weird hero, most of which were written by Walter Gibson.

184. Rogers, Alva. *A Requiem for Astounding.* Chicago: Advent, 1964. 224pp.

A nostalgic history of *Astounding Science Fiction* magazine from its birth as *Astounding Stories of Super-Science* in 1930 until its metamorphosis into *Analog* in 1960. Excessively detailed, yet preserves useful information.

185. Weinberg, Robert. *The Weird Tales Story*. West Linn,
    OR: FAX Collector's Editions, 1977. 134pp.

An informal and disorganized history of *Weird Tales*
(1923-1954), the most influential fantasy magazine
of the 1920s and 1930s. The focus of the book is a
chronological study of the pulp's content divided
into three chapters which discuss the fiction, the
cover art, and the interior art. These chapters incorporate biographical sketches of the contributing
authors and artists, as well as some historical detail and an interview with cover artist Margaret
Brundage. E. Hoffmann Price's disappointing chapter
on editor Farnsworth Wright is more of an autobiographical fragment than a study of his subject. Recollections of the magazine are provided by Frank
Belknap Long, H. Warner Munn, Robert Bloch, and
others (many of whom were previously printed in
Weinberg's *WT 50: A Tribute to Weird Tales*). Tone
and arrangement of contents adversely affect the
usefulness of this volume. The book is poorly organized and lacks historical perspective--the limited
literary evaluation makes no attempt to relate the
pulp or its contents to a wider literary tradition.
Inadequate references, lack of a checklist of the
pulp and its contents, and no index combine to make
this book unsuitable for scholarly use.

5. Book Reviews

186. Hall, H.W. *Science Fiction Book Review Index, 1923-
    1973*. Detroit: Gale Research, 1975. 438pp.

A complete record of books reviewed in science fiction and fantasy magazines from 1923 to 1973. Beginning in 1970, coverage is expanded to include general, library, and amateur magazines as well as
specialized sources like *Extrapolation* and *Foundation*. Provides access to approximately 14,000 reviews
of 6900 books. Appendices include a complete record
of the SF and fantasy magazines 1923-1976 (which
provides an issue-by-issue checklist of each as well
as other data), a title checklist of the general,
library, and amateur magazines, a checklist of the
major SF indices, and an index of magazine editors.
Books reviewed are indexed by author and title.
This work supersedes the less comprehensive *An Index
to the Science Fiction Book Reviews in Astounding/
Analog, 1949-1969, Fantasy and Science Fiction, 1949-
1969, Galaxy, 1950-1969*, compiled by Barry McGhan
and others and issued in 1973. Due to the lack of

an extensive body of SF criticism concentrating on
individual authors or titles, this book is an indispensible reference aid. Annual supplements were issued covering the 1974 and 1975 reviews.

6. Film

187. Baxter, John. *Science Fiction in the Cinema*.
     London: Zwemmer, 1970. 240pp. [paper]. Also
     New York: A.S. Barnes, 1970. [paper].

     A history of the SF film from 1895 to 1968. The
     coverage is broad and informed, especially for the
     period 1900 to 1940. Includes a chapter on SF for
     television. Contains a bibliography which includes
     critical works on the fantastic cinema and a select
     filmography.

188. Brosnan, John. *The Horror People*. New York: St.
     Martin's Press, 1976. 304pp.

     Not a historical survey of the horror film, but
     a look at the people who have influenced the horror
     film genre. The work is divided into three sections:
     the actors--the Chaneys, Bela Lugosi, Boris Karloff--
     whose names became synonymous with early horror films,
     and directors--Tod Browning, Karl Freund, James
     Whale--whose work was most influential in the crea-
     tion and development of the genre from the 1920s
     through the 1940s; the major influences of the 1950s
     --the work of Jack Arnold and William Castle and the
     productions of Hammer and American International;
     and the careers of the modern masters--Vincent Price,
     Christopher Lee, and Peter Cushing. The final por-
     tion of the book contains interviews with writers,
     directors, producers, and horror fans, and an appen-
     dix contains brief biographies of additional "horror
     people."

189. Clarens, Carlos. *An Illustrated History of the
     Horror Film*. New York: Capricorn Books, 1967.
     256pp. [paper].

     A useful critical history of the horror and SF film
     from 1895 through the mid-1960s. A 69-page appendix
     provides cast and credits of films mentioned in the
     text. Indexed.

190. Gerani, Gary with Paul H. Schulman. *Fantastic Tele-*
     vision. New York: Harmony Books, 1977. 192pp.
     [paper].

     A useful survey of SF and fantasy TV series from
     Captain Video to Star Trek and Space 1999. Part One
     focuses upon thirteen of the most distinctive and
     memorable series and provides a brief history and
     analysis of each, plus an index of episodes (with
     credits, cast, and plot summaries). Part Two is a
     comprehensive, but not exhaustive, listing (with
     brief summaries) of American and British TV fantasy
     series, juvenile series, and made-for-TV movies. A
     competent survey, with intelligent and perceptive
     commentary, of nearly thirty years of TV fantasy.
     Indexed.

191. Johnson, William, ed. *Focus on the Science Fiction*
     Film. Englewood Cliffs, NJ: Prentice-Hall, 1972.
     182pp.

     Essays by American, British and European critics on
     the SF film and its relation to other films and SF
     literature covering three historical periods: 1895-
     1940, the 1950s, and the 1960s. Includes a chron-
     ology, selective filmography, annotated bibliography
     of book and periodical criticism, and index.

192. Menville, Douglas. *A Historical and Critical Survey*
     of the Science-Fiction Film. New York: Arno Press,
     1975. 185pp.

     A reprint of the author's M.A. thesis at the Univer-
     sity of Southern California in 1959, the work is
     divided into three sections: the first is a brief
     survey of science fiction literature; the second is
     an examination of the fantastic film beginning with
     the pioneering work of George Melies; and the con-
     cluding section is a critical examination of the
     merits and failings of the science fiction film. An
     appendix lists SF films produced throughout the world
     between 1900 and 1957. This work is not very analyti-
     cal and tends to be a tedious catalog of the SF film
     with plot summaries, but there are a number of quo-
     tations, adequately referenced, and useful appendices
     which make this book a useful beginning point for
     science fiction critical film study.

193. Rovin, Jeff. *The Fabulous Fantasy Films*. New York:
     A.S. Barnes, 1977. 271pp.

     The most comprehensive study of the fantasy film,
     from *Nosferatu* and *Cabinet of Dr. Caligari* to the

recent *Sinbad in the Eye of the Tiger*. Includes discussion of over 600 films which are arranged by thematic content, plus chapters on fantasy animation,
fantasy film anthologies, and TV fantasy. Appendix 1
lists cast and credits of 500 famtasy films; Appendix 2 comprises interviews with people involved in
the creation of fantasy films. Indexed.

194. Strick, Philip. *Science Fiction Movies*. London:
Octopus Books, 1976. 160pp.

"The best book so far on SF and the cinema. . . .
Heavy emphasis on the pictorial, but there is still
space for about 70,000 words of text. . . . Excellent
balance between word and picture. Although Strick
does not flaunt his research work, it must have been
very considerable. He lists many more films than any
previous work in the field (except, of course, for
Walt Lee's extraordinarily thorough three volume
filmography), and gives the impression of having
seen most of them. . . . The book is clearly written
by an 'intellectual,' but it is not elitist."
[Not seen, extracts quoted from a review by Peter
Nicholls in *Foundation*, 11/12.]

IV. AUTHOR STUDIES & BIBLIOGRAPHIES

A. COLLECTIVE

195. Aldiss, Brian W. and Harry Harrison, eds. *Hell's Cartographers: Some Personal Histories of Science Fiction Writers*. London: Weidenfield and Nicolson, 1975. 246pp.

Autobiographical sketches by six post-war science fiction writers: Alfred Bester, Damon Knight, Frederik Pohl, Robert Silverberg, Harry Harrison, and Brian W. Aldiss. Checklists and photographs of the six authors.

196. Clareson, Thomas D., ed. *Voices for the Future: Essays on Major Science Fiction Writers*. Bowling Green, OH: Bowling Green University Popular Press, 1976. 283pp.

A collection of critical essays which, for the most part, concern writers of science fiction whose careers had begun by the end of World War II. Following a general introductory survey by Jack Williamson on magazine publishing in the 1930s and 1940s are articles focusing on Jack Williamson, Olaf Stapledon, Clifford Simak, Isaac Asimov, Robert Heinlein, Theodore Sturgeon, Ray Bradbury (two essays), Arthur Clarke, Kurt Vonnegut, Henry Kuttner, and C.L. Moore. This book fills a void in science fiction scholarship, that of the single-author study. Each essay deals with an interpretation of the major works of the subject writer set against the the writer's general background.

197. Day, Bradford M. *Bibliography of Adventure: Mundy, Burroughs, Rohmer, Haggard*. Denver, NY: Science Fiction and Fantasy Publications, 1964. 125pp. [paper].

The checklists of Edgar Rice Burroughs, Talbot Munday, and Sax Rohmer are revised from their earlier versions as separate pamphlets issued in 1962, 1955, and 1963 respectfully.

198. Ellis, S.M. *Wilkie Collins, Le Fanu and Others*.
     London: Constable, 1931. 343pp.

     Bibliographical studies with comprehensive bibli-
     ographies of British authors who were at their peak
     in the mid-19th century. These studies are "personal
     rather than critical, and seek to show the influence
     of heredity, early environment, scenery, places of
     residence, and actual experiences upon the writers'
     literary work." Subjects are: Wilkie Collins, Char-
     les Allston Collins, Mortimer Collins, R.D. Black-
     more, Joseph Sheridan Le Fanu, Edward Bradley and
     George Lawrence, Mary Ann and Thomas Hughes, John
     Crossley (a bibliophile), and Mrs. J.H. Riddell.
     Germane to the study of fantastic literature is the
     chapter on Le Fanu which contains important bio-
     graphical data not easily located elsewhere and an
     extensive bibliography which includes magazine con-
     tributions as well as published books.

199. Hillegas, Mark R., ed. *Shadows of Imagination: The
     Fantasies of C.S. Lewis, J.R.R. Tolkien, and
     Charles Williams*. Carbondale: Southern Illinois
     University Press, 1969. 170pp. Rpt. 1976 [paper].

     Essays by academic critics on the works of three
     important fantasists. This book evolved from a
     seminar on Lewis and Tolkien at the 1966 MLA Annual
     Meeting. The three writers treated here are regarded
     as "serious fantasists" who share a belief in fan-
     tasy as "a mode valuable for presenting moral or
     spiritual values, which could not be presented in
     realistic fiction: a way of transcending the limit-
     ations of human existence to attain new perspectives
     and insights."

200. Manlove, C.N. *Modern Fantasy: Five Studies*. Cam-
     bridge, MA and London: Cambridge University
     Press, 1975. 308pp.

     A literary analysis of five modern fantasists and
     their major works: Charles Kingsley (*The Water-
     Babies*), George MacDonald, C.S. Lewis (*Perelandra*),
     J.R.R. Tolkien (*The Lord of the Rings*), and Mervyn
     Peake (The Titus Trilogy). Each analysis is set in
     an illustrative context of the writer's life,
     thought, and other works.

201. Purtill, Richard. *Lord of Elves and Eldils: Fantasy
     and Philosophy in C.S. Lewis and J.R.R. Tolkien*.
     Grand Rapids, MI: Zondervan, 1974. 216pp. [paper].

A study of Lewis and Tolkien which contrasts their
themes and styles within the framework of fantasy,
style, language, and philosophy. Appendices contain
a selected bibliography of fiction and criticism
and a discussion of literature which influenced or
was influenced by the work of Lewis and Tolkien.
Indexed.

202. Samuelson, David. *Visions of Tomorrow: Six Journeys
     from Outer to Inner Space.* New York: Arno Press,
     1975. 429pp.

A reprint of the author's Ph.D. dissertation at the
University of Southern California, 1969, this book
is an intensive study of six novels representative
of American and British science fiction in the per-
iod following World War II: *The Caves of Steel* by
Isaac Asimov, *The Crystal World* by J.G. Ballard,
Rogue Moon by Algis Budrys, *Childhood's End* by
Arthur C. Clarke, *A Canticle for Leibowitz* by Walter
M. Miller, Jr., and *More Than Human* by Theodore
Sturgeon. An important pioneer study of post-World
War II science fiction, and the first extended and
detailed examination of individual SF novels. The
first 83 pages comprise a good historical survey of
the genre.

203. Schweitzer, Darrell, ed. *SF Voices.* Baltimore: T-K
     Graphics, 1976. 123pp. [paper].

A collection of fourteen interviews, some of which
originally appeared in professional and amateur
magazines. Interviewed are: Alfred Bester, Robert
Silverberg, Brian Aldiss, James Gunn, Gardner Dozois,
Norman Spinrad, Gordon Dickson, Ben Bova, Ted White,
Jack Williamson, L. Sprague de Camp, Frank Belknap
Long, Gahan Wilson, and Jerry Pournelle.

204. Tuck, Donald H. *Authors' Books Listing.* Lindisfarne,
     Australia: By the Author, 1975. 32pp. [paper].

Checklists of hardcover and paperback books by seven
science fiction writers: John Brunner, A. Bertram
Chandler, Edmund Cooper, Philip Jose Farmer, Ursula
K. Le Guin, Michael Moorcock, and A.E. Van Vogt.
The booklet was prepared for the 33rd World Science
Fiction Convention at Melbourne, 14-17 August, 1975.

205. Tuck, Donald H. *Author's Works Listing.* Hobart,
     Tasmania: By the Author, 1960-62. 121pp. [un-
     bound].

A series of 21 checklists issued in three series
covering hardcover and paperbound books, magazine
fiction and series listings of subject writers.
Authors included are: Isaac Asimov, Nelson S. Bond,
Fredric Brown, Hal Clement, Ray Cummings, Robert A.
Heinlein, Damon Knight, Stanley G. Weinbaum, Poul
Anderson, Arthur C. Clarke, David H. Keller, Otis
Adelbert Kline, Murray Leinster, Nathan Schachner,
Henry S. Whitehead, August Derleth (SF and fantasy
fiction only), Edmond Hamilton, Cyril M. Kornbluth,
Frank Belknap Long, Eric Frank Russell, and Clifford
D. Simak. The format is similar to Tuck's *The Ency-
clopedia of Science Fiction and Fantasy,* and much
of the data will be updated and superseded when that
work is published in its entirety. At present, this
series contains details not readily located elsewhere.

206. Urang, Gunnar. *Shadows of Heaven: Religion and Fan-
      tasy in the Writings of C.S. Lewis, Charles
      Williams, and J.R.R. Tolkien.* Philadelphia:
      Pilgrim Press, 1971. 186pp.

A study of the impact of the fantasy writings of
Lewis, Williams and Tolkien upon literature and
theology. One chapter is devoted to each author,
with a concluding chapter which attempts to inter-
relate the various works examined to the larger
question of "can the pattern of belief represented
by the work be considered adequate to the experience
and the developing consciousness of modern man?" A
Christian approach to Lewis, Williams and Tolkien
which explores the themes and attitudes of fantasy,
grace, and romantic love.

B. INDIVIDUAL

BRIAN W. ALDISS

207. Aldiss, Margaret. *Item Eighty-Three: Brian W. Aldiss,
      1954-1972.* Oxford: Bocardo Press, 1973. 40pp.
      [paper].

An expanded version of a checklist first published
in 1962 as *Item Forty-Three: Brian W. Aldiss, A
Bibliography, 1954-1962.* A detailed three-part bibliography of Aldiss' fiction, non-fiction, and edited
works. Some items in the 1962 edition were annotated
by Aldiss, but these comments were deleted from the
1973 printing.

HANS CHRISTIAN ANDERSEN

208. Bredsdorff, Elias. *Hans Christian Andersen: The Story of His Life and Work 1805-75.* New York: Charles Scribner's Sons, 1975. 376pp.

    The fullest biography in any language and the culmination of the author's lifelong study and enjoyment of the "unsurpassed master" of the fairy tale. Makes extensive use of Andersen's journals, correspondence, notebooks, and other primary source material. The second part of the book, a study of the fairy tales, will be a revelation to most people, for, as the author states, Andersen has long been relegated to the nursery, and few adults realize the full extent of his with, charm, and sheer genius. Extensive bibliography of primary materials. Indexed.

ISAAC ASIMOV

209. Goble, Neil. *Asimov Analyzed.* Baltimore: Mirage Press, 1972. 174pp.

    A detailed analysis of Asimov's literary style with emphasis on his scientific writing. Of value for its analysis of Asimov's writing style and summaries of content of his non-fiction works; but Patrouch's *The Science Fiction of Isaac Asimov* is more germane to the study of the science fiction. Contains a bibliography (detailing contents) of Asimov's first 100 books, but Miller's *Isaac Asimov: A Checklist* is the preferred bibliography. Indexed.

210. Miller, Marjorie M. *Isaac Asimov: A Checklist of Works Published in the United States, March 1939-May 1972.* [Kent, OH]: Kent State University Press, 1972. 98pp.

    Part one is a chronological checklist of fiction and non-fiction published in English language books and periodicals as of mid-1972. Detailed entries provide information on initial and subsequent appearances. Indexed by title. Part two is a brief annotated checklist (28 entries) of selected criticism and works about Asimov. Currently, the most comprehensive Asimov bibliography.

211. Patrouch, Joseph F., Jr. *The Science Fiction of Isaac Asimov.* Garden City: Doubleday, 1974. 283pp.

A critical analysis of all of Asimov's fiction. A perceptive study which provides an excellent comparison of Asimov's themes and literary style. Patrouch makes no attempt to deal with science fiction in general (though occasional references occur) nor to place Asimov's writings in the wider literary tradition.

JAMES GRAHAM BALLARD

212. Goddard, James and David Pringle, eds. *J.G. Ballard: The First Twenty Years*. Hayes, England: Bran's Head Books, 1976. 99pp.

Concerns the work and literary career of one of the most influential literary figures to arise from the science fiction genre. Following the introductory essay by the editors is a twenty-eight page interview with Ballard recorded 4 January 1975. The focus of the book is on the symposium, comprising seven essays and reviews. Contents: "The Wounded Land: J.G. Ballard" by Brian W. Aldiss, "The Fourfold Symbolism of J.G. Ballard" by David Pringle, "Modern Metaphors" by Michael Moorcock, "An Honest Madness" by Pringle, "The Greening of Ballard" by Ian Watson, "Review of *Concrete Island*" by Peter Linnett, and "The Incredible Shrinking World: A Review of J.G. Ballard's *High-Rise*" by Pringle. Contains a detailed chronological bibliography (including reprint data and content listing) of published fiction (this section cross-referenced with an alphabetical index), translations of works into foreign languages (not comprehensive), and non-fiction.

L. FRANK BAUM

213. Baum, Frank Joslyn and Russell P. McFall. *To Please a Child*. Chicago: Reilly and Lee, 1962. 284pp.

To date, the major biographical source on Baum, partially intended as a memoir by a son.

214. Baum, Joan and Ronald Baughman. *L. Frank Baum: The Wonderful Wizard of Oz. An Exhibition of His Published Writings, in Commemoration of the Centenary of His Birth, May 15, 1856*. New York: Columbia University Libraries, 1956. 50pp. [paper].

A catalogue of 112 items—books and ephemeral material, letters, and drawings (by W.W. Denslow)—by, about, or relating to Baum exhibited in the Columbia University Libraries, January 16-March 16, 1956. Divided into five sections: the Oz books (only those by Baum); other books for children; series books for children and young adults; books for adults and miscellanea; and biography and criticism. Useful bibliographical data is provided, but the main value of the compilation is the extensive historical and descriptive annotations provided each entry.

215. Gardner, Martin and Russel B. Nye. *The Wizard of Oz and Who He Was*. East Lansing: Michigan State University Press, 1957. 208pp.

The first extensive contribution to Baum scholarship. In addition to the two essays by Gardner and Nye, the volume includes a partially annotated edition of the *Wizard*, as well as the first attempt at a comprehensive bibliography covering the writings of Baum.

216. Hanff, Peter E. and Douglas G. Greene. *Bibliographia Oziana: A Concise Bibliographical Checklist of the Oz Books by L. Frank Baum and His Successors*. Demorest, GA: International Wizard of Oz Club, 1976. 103pp. [paper].

A descriptive bibliography of the 43 Oz books of Baum, Ruth Plumly Thompson, John R. Neill, Jack Snow, Rachel R. Cosgrove and Eloise Jarvis McGraw, and Lauren McGraw Wagner, as well as associational books by W.W. Denslow and Frank Joslyn Baum. In addition to textual facsimiles, there are 82 photographic illustrations of book covers and dust jackets. This compilation will probably remain the definitive bibliographical study of the Oz books for some time. Additional bibliographical and historical data on the writings of Baum will be found in *The Annotated Wizard of Oz. . . With an Introduction, Notes and Bibliography by Michael Patrick Hearn* (New York: Clarkson N. Potter, 1973). In addition to the valuable 70-page historical introduction, this work includes a chapter on illustrator W.W. Denslow and an extensive annotated checklist of Baum's writings, including: books and pamphlets, anonymous and pseudonymous books, published songs, produced and directed plays, introductions and other contributions, short stories and poems, and notable later editions and translations and foreign editions of *The Wizard of Oz*.

217. Moore, Raylyn. *Wonderful Wizard, Marvelous Land*.
Bowling Green, OH: Bowling Green University
Popular Press, 1974. 213pp.

A study of Baum's life, art, a detailed analysis of
the Oz books, and an analysis of their literary impact and value. Includes a partially annotated primary bibliography and a selected secondary list of
critical and biographical sources.

ROBERT BLOCH

218. Hall, Graham. *Robert Bloch Bibliography*. Tewkes-
bury, Gloucestershire: Graham M. Hall, 1965.
31pp. [paper].

A checklist of Bloch's published fiction and non-
fiction appearing in books and professional magazines
from 1935 through 1964. For part one the listing is
strictly chronological with collections, reprints,
and foreign editions interfiled by date. Part two
is a listing of periodical contributions arranged
alphabetically by magazine. As there is no alphabetical cross index, locating material takes diligent
searching. This is regretable, as there is much useful data here.

ANTHONY BOUCHER (WILLIAM ANTHONY PARKER WHITE)

219. Offord, Lenore Glen, comp. *A Boucher Portrait:
Anthony Boucher as Seen by his Friends and
Colleagues. . . And A.* [sic] *Boucher Bibli-
ograpgy Compiled by J.R. Christopher with D.W.
Dickensheet and R.E. Briney.* White Bear Lake,
MN: The Armchair Detective, n.d.

Tributes and bibliography originally appearing
in *The Armchair Detective*, vol. 2, nos. 2-4.
The detailed and heavily annotated bibliography
includes book and magazine appearances of fiction
and non-fiction, both professional and amateur.

RAY BRADBURY

220. Indick, Benjamin P. *The Drama of Ray Bradbury*.
Baltimore: T-K Graphics, 1977. 23pp. [paper].

A short, but useful study of Bradbury's original
dramatic works and adaptations of his writings for
radio, film, and stage. A checklist of published
plays is included.

221. Nolan, William F. *The Ray Bradbury Companion: A Life
     and Career History, Photolog, and Comprehensive
     Checklist of Writings With Facsimiles From Ray
     Bradbury's Unpublished and Uncollected Work in
     all Media.* Detroit: Gale Research, 1975. 339pp.

This visually impressive book provides a wealth of
data on a writer who has produced what is perhaps
the single best-known 20th century science fiction
book, *The Martian Chronicles.* Although most readers
think of Bradbury as a writer of fiction, he has
authored at least 150 non-fiction pieces, including
verse, plays, essays, reviews, and scripts. Nolan
has spent 23 years gathering and recording the more
than 700 original works by a writer whose SF is seminal to the genre and which, through its breadth,
philosophy, and style, has been instrumental in
bringing modern SF back into the literary mainstream.
The comprehensive checklist, profusely illustrated
with facsimiles of book covers, dust jackets, title
pages, and other items, includes books and pamphlets,
his magazine, fiction, articles and other non-fiction, verse, introductions, reviews, published speeches, published plays, stage productions, films, television, radio, published letters, interviews, anthology appearances, comic book appearances, recordings, dedications, and pseudonyms, as well as writings about him in books, periodicals, newspapers,
and graduate research. In addition, there is a lengthy
record of his life and career in chronological format, facsimiles of his unpublished and uncollected
work in all media, a photolog, and an introduction
by Bradbury. Corrigenda, additions, and an update of
bibliographical material will be found in articles
by Donn Albright in *Xenophile*, nos. 13 and 26.

222. Slusser, George Edgar. *The Bradbury Chronicles.*
     San Bernardino, CA: Borgo Press, 1977. 64pp.
     [paper].

A critical analysis of Bradbury's fiction. A useful
study, especially for the short synopses of numerous
short stories.

223. Breen, Walter. *The Gemini Problem: A Study in Dark-over*. Berkeley: By the Author, 1973. [pagination not known] [paper]. Rpt. Baltimore: T-K Graphics, 1976. 39pp. [paper].

A brief study of Bradley's Darkover novels, including a discussion of the style, framework, and themes of the series.

224. Wise, S. *The Darkover Dilemma: Problems of the Darkover Series*. Baltimore: T-K Graphics, 1976. 28pp. [paper].

A brief look at the Darkover novels with identification of some of the contradictions in content and theme.

JOHN BRUNNER

225. De Bolt, Joe, ed. *The Happening Worlds of John Brunner*. Port Washington, NY: Kennikat Press, 1975. 216pp.

A collection of interdisciplinary essays by academics from the humanities, the social sciences, and the physical sciences, which examine Brunner's work for such qualities as technological accuracy and political radicalism as well as literary precedents and style. De Bolt's lengthy career biography and Brunner's own concluding response add dimension to the work. Preface by James Blish and seven essays: "Brunner's Novels: A Posterity for Kipling" by John R. Pfeiffer, "John Brunner's Short Fiction: The More Things Change. . ." by Stephen C. Holder, "'It Goes Bang': Structure of Rhythms in the Poetry" by Ronald Primeau, "The Future of Empire: Conflict in the Major Fiction of John Brunner" by Norman Rasulis, "Government and Politics in Selected Works of John Brunner" by William P. Browne, "Sic Pavis Magna: Science, Technology, and Ecology in John Brunner's Science Fiction" by Rober R. Slocum, and "The Computer and Man: The Human Use of Non-Human Beings in the Works of John Brunner" by Edward L. Lamie and Joe De Bolt. Appended is an extensive bibliography of Brunner's published fiction and non-fiction published in English language books and periodicals, as well as selected works about him.

ANTHONY BURGESS (ANTHONY BURGESS WILSON)

226. Boytinck, Paul. *Anthony Burgess: An Enumerative Bibliography with Selected Annotations*. Norwood, PA: Norwood Editions, 1974. 43pp.

A partially annotated checklist of Burgess' published fiction and non-fiction, including articles, essays, and reviews, as well as books in foreign translation. In addition, there are entries for works about Burgess, including graduate research, articles, and essays in books and periodicals, as well as reviews of his books. The compiler admits to lack of personal examination of some of the material (these are not indicated), a grevious fault in any bibliographical undertaking; and brevity or lack of annotation and sketchy bibliographic details on many entries additionally limit the usefulness of this work.

EDGAR RICE BURROUGHS

227. Harwood, John. *The Literature of Burroughsiana: A Listing of Magazine Articles, Book Commentaries, News Items, Book Reviews, Movie Reviews, Fanzines, Amateur Publications, and Related Items Concerning the Life and/or Works of Edgar Rice Burroughs*. Baton Rouge, LA: Camille Cazedessus, 1963. 105pp. [paper].

The culmination of 24 years of research by the compiler, this listing of more than 1000 items covering over forty years of commentary on Burroughs and his works is arranged into six categories with entries in each section listed chronologically. A valuable supplement to Hein's *A Golden Anniversary Bibliography of Edgar Rice Burroughs*.

228. Heins, Henry Hardy. *A Golden Anniversary Bibliography of Edgar Rice Burroughs*. West Kingston, RI: Donald M. Grant, 1964. 418pp.

Still the standard bibliography of the writings of Burroughs. A revision of the author's privately printed 122-page version, issued in an edition of 150 copies in 1962. It identifies in detail all the known book and magazine versions of Burroughs' work, including information for the identification of first editions and reprints of his books. The volume includes pictorial reproductions of all the full-page publisher's advertisements for the novels as they appeared in *Publishers Weekly* from 1914 to 1948 (as well as other sources to 1963), the magazine artwork of J. Allen St. John (whose work is closely associated with Burroughs' fiction), and additional material, including five articles by ERB. For those lacking access to this work, P.H. Adkins' *Edgar Rice Burroughs: Bibliography & Price Guide* (New Orleans: P.D.A. Enterprises, 1974) is a brief, but up-to-date and useful substitute.

229. Lupoff, Richard A. *Barsoom: Edgar Rice Burroughs and the Martian Vision*. Baltimore: Mirage Press, 1976. 161pp.

A critical study of the eleven works which comprise the Martian cycle, with emphasis on analysis and evaluation rather than on description. No index.

230. Lupoff, Richard A. *Edgar Rice Burroughs: Master of Adventure*. New York: Canaveral Press, 1965. 297pp. Rev. ed. New York: Ace Books, 1968. [paper]. Rpt. 1975. 317pp. [paper].

The first book-length study of Burroughs and his work, with emphasis on his writings. Commentary on his fiction is here more descriptive than analytical. The first edition is indexed; regretably the paperback printings are not.

231. Porges, Irwin. *Edgar Rice Burroughs: The Man Who Created Tarzan*. Provo, UT: Brigham Young University Press, 1975. 819pp.

An extensive, possibly definitive biography of Burroughs. Porges devoted four years to researching this volume with full access to the vast accumulation of records, letters, photos, and family documents housed at Tarzana, as well as interviews with surviving members of the Burroughs family, including his children, children-in-law, and his second wife. Appendices include geneological data, an autobiographical sketch by ERB, reminiscences of Hulbert Burroughs, and a complete listing of Burroughs' writings. Indexed.

232. Roy, John Flint. *A Guide to Barsoom: Eleven Sections of References in One Volume Dealing with the Martian Stories Written by Edgar Rice Burroughs*. New York: Ballantine Books, 1976. 200pp. [paper].

A compendium of Barsoomian lore gleaned from the novels comprising the Martian cycle. A gazeteer, biographical dictionary, survey of flora and fauna,

and a study of religions, customs, civilization and
scientific avhievements of the inhabitants of the
Mars of ERB.

WILLIAM SEWARD BURROUGHS

233. Goodman, Michael B. *William S. Burroughs: An Annotated Bibliography of His Works and Criticism.*
New York: Garland Publishing, 1975. 96pp.

An annotated bibliography of published and unpublished material by and about Burroughs. Lists books,
magazine fiction, articles, and essays by Burroughs;
interviews, and biographical and critical material
about him. Also includes letters (with abstracts)
housed at Columbia University and a description of
the Grove Press archive at Syracuse University. Researchers deeply committed to the study of William
Burroughs should also consult *A Descriptive Catalogue of the William S. Burroughs Archive, Compiled
by Miles Associates for William Burroughs and Brion
Gysin* (London: Covent Garden Press, 1973), which
describes, with partial annotations, an archive of
over 14,000 books, manuscript pages, proofs, letters,
and other material, mostly from the period 1958
through 1971.

JAMES BRANCH CABELL

234. Brewer, Frances Joan. *James Branch Cabell: A Bibli-
ography of His Writings, Biography and Criticism.*
Charlottesville, VA: University of Virginia
Press, 1957. 206pp.

A descriptive bibliography of the writings in English language books and periodicals, including fiction, biography, introductions, essays, criticism,
reviews, etc. Part one lists books by subject classification (i.e., "Biography of the Life of Manuel,"
"Virginians Are Various," etc.), but for ease of
access they are organized chronologically elsewhere
as well. Part two lists Cabell's contributions to
books and magazines and is arranged alphabetically
by title. Part three lists biographical and critical
material by and about him. Extensive index.

235. Bruccoli, Matthew J. *Notes on the Cabell Collection at the University of Virginia*. Charlottesville, VA: University of Virginia Press, 1957. 178pp.

This study was planned as a companion volume to Brewer's *James Branch Cabell: A Bibliography*, and follows her ordering of Cabell's books. The work comprises a listing of all the impressions of all the editions of Cabell's works in the Alderman Library of the University of Virginia. Additionally, it includes descriptions of manuscripts and setting copies as well as letters (mostly addressed to Guy Holt, an early Cabell bibliographer, and the novelist Ellen Glasgow). Indexed.

236. Davis, Joe Lee. *James Branch Cabell*. New York: Twayne Publishers, 1962. 174pp.

This study concentrates on a "thematic and formal analysis of each of Cabell's sequence works in the shape, and approximately in the order, their author finally designed them for reading."

237. Hall, James N. *James Branch Cabell: A Complete Bibliography*. New York: Revisionist Press, 1974. 245pp.

A descriptive bibliography of Cabell's works, organized into three parts: Part one lists Cabell's books; Part two lists Cabell's contributions to periodicals, material appearing in forms other than periodicals, and reprint material; Part three lists books and pamphlets about Cabell and his works, including bibliographies, Cabellian art, and Cabellian magazines. An appendix furnishes some of the locations where the various editions of Cabell's books may be found; a second appendix (by Nelson Bond) lists the current (1974) retail values of all Cabell books.

JOHN W. CAMPBELL, JR.

238. Bangsund, John, ed. *John W. Campbell: An Australian Tribute*. Canberra: Ronald E. Graham and John Bangsund, 1972. 100pp. [paper].

A volume of tributes and memoirs, plus the transcript of a symposium on Campbell held at the University of Melbourne, 16 September 1971 under the sponsorship of the Melbourne University Science Fiction Association. Also prints the text of two letters from Campbell to Jack Wodhams and Ronald E. Graham. The bib-

liography of Campbell, compiled by Donald Tuck,
lists books, series, and short fiction, but omits
edited books and non-fiction. Indexed.

LEWIS CARROLL (CHARLES LUTWIDGE DODGSON)

239. Gattegno, Jean. *Lewis Carroll: Fragments of a
     Looking Glass*. New York: Thomas Y. Crowell,
     1976. 327pp.

An expert on Charles L. Dodgson here expands an
earlier text published in 1970. Gattegno has had
access to the diaries kept by Dodgson as well as
to other source material. Includes "A Carroll Chronology" followed by a brief summing up of the pattern
of Dodgson's life. A select bibliography is useful
for the French titles.

240. Hudson, Derek. *Lewis Carroll*. London: Constable,
     1954. 354pp.

An excellent study, the first since Collingwood
(*The Life and Letters of Lewis Carroll,* 1889) to
make use of the Dodgson diaries, is the nearest
approach to a definitive biography that has been
published to date.

241. Williams, Sidney Herbert and Falconer Madan. *The
     Lewis Carroll Handbook: Being a New Version of
     the Literature of the Rev. C.L. Dodgson. . .
     Now Revised, Augmented and Brought Up to 1960
     by Roger Lancelyn Green*. London: Oxford Univer-
     sity Press, 1962. 307pp.

The definitive descriptive bibliography of the writings of Lewis Carroll, being an extensive revision
and enlargement of *A Handbook of the Literature of
the Rev. C.L. Dodgson (Lewis Carroll),* by Williams
and Madan, which, upon first publication in 1931,
established itself as a sort of "Bible" for Carrol-
lians. Part one is a list, with notes, of all pieces
and editions printed or issued by Dodgson from 1845
to 1898 and editions of his work containing new material or reprints of exceptional interest from 1898
to 1960, in order of date. Part two comprises notes
of ordinary editions of his works issued from 1898
to 1960, with American editions of any date. Part
three is a listing of material about Dodgson, including memoirs, reminiscences, memorials, criticism,
bibliographies, etc. in books and periodicals. Indexed.

GILBERT KEITH CHESTERTON

242. Boyd, Ian. *The Novels of G.K. Chesterton: A Study in Art and Propaganda*. New York: Barnes & Noble, 1975. 241pp.

A literary study of eleven novels "which form the largest and most coherent part of. . . his achievement as a writer." Focuses on the political and social themes.

243. Clipper, Lawrence J. *G.K. Chesterton*. New York: Twayne, 1974. 190pp.

A literary biography which includes information on Chesterton's works and his career as a critic and man of letters. Includes a chronology and a selected bibliography of primary and secondary materials.

244. Sullivan, John. *G.K. Chesterton: A Bibliography*. London: University of London Press, 1958. 208pp. Rpt. Westport, CT: Greenwood Press, 1974.

A descriptive bibliography of Chesterton's works divided into the following categories: books and pamphlets, contributions to books and pamphlets, contributions to periodicals, books and articles about Chesterton, collections and selections, translations into foreign languages of books by Chesterton. The titles are arranged chronologically in each category. Comprehensive index.

245. Sullivan, John, ed. *G.K. Chesterton: A Centenary Appraisal*. New York: Barnes & Noble, 1974. 243pp.

An anthology of critical essays on Chesterton's life, reputation, abllity, and influence. Contents: "A Brief Survey of Chesterton's Work" by Dudley Parker, "Chesterton the Edwardian" by P.N. Furbank, "Four Fluent Fellows: An Essay on Chesterton's Fiction" by Kingsley Amis, "Philosophy in Fiction" by Ian Boyd, "Father Brown and Others" by W.W. Robson, "The Gift of Wonder" by W.H. Auden, "The Achievement of G.K. Chesterton" by Stephen Medcalf, "G.K. Chesterton, Journalist" by G.C. Heseltine, "Devereux Nights: A Distributist Memoir" by Brocard Sewell, "Recollections" by Dorothy E. Collins, "A Liberal Education" by John Sullivan, "Chesterton and the Future of Democracy" by Patrick Cahill, "Chesterton in France" by Christine d'Haussy, and "Chesterton in Japan" by Peter Milward.

LESTER DENT

246. Weinberg, Robert, ed. *The Man Behind Doc Savage: A Tribute to Lester Dent*. Oak Lawn, IL: Robert Weinberg, 1974. 127pp. [paper].

A collection of essays on Dent's fiction, emphasizing his popular super hero, Doc Savage. Includes a biographical sketch by Weinberg, and an essay by Philip Jose Farmer on his "biography," *Doc Savage: His Apocalyptic Life*. Also present are two fictions by Dent as well as his analysis of the pulp magazine master plot. No bibliographies or index, both of which would have been useful.

AUGUST DERLETH

247. Derleth, August. *100 Books by August Derleth*. Sauk City, WI: Arkham House, 1962. 121pp.

A checklist of Derleth's published writings in books and periodicals, intended as a record and a promotional piece on the occasion of his 100th book (although the checklist includes 102 titles). The checklist of published books includes information on contents, publication data, and reprints. Includes a listing of magazines, newspapers, and "occasional reference works in cloth covers" which contained short stories, essays, reviews, miscellaneous prose, and poetry, but no indication of contribution or issue. Also lists recordings, compilations, book introductions, appearances in anthologies and textbooks, and other material.

PHILIP K. DICK

248. Gillespie, Bruce, ed. *Philip K. Dick: Electric Shepherd*. Melbourne, Australia: Nostrilla Press, 1975. 106pp. [paper].

A collection of critical essays on the science fiction of Dick by Stanislaw Lem and others, with introductory comment by Roger Zelazny and responses by Dick, as well as his speech, "The Android and the Human," collected from *SF Commentary*. Also features a checklist of Dick's published book and magazine fiction compiled by Fred Patten. Indexed.

249. Taylor, Angus. *Philip K. Dick & The Umbrella of
    Light*. Baltimore: T-K Graphics, 1975. 52pp.
    [paper].

    A critical analysis of Dick's science fiction
    based in part on an earlier study, "Can God Fly?
    Can He Hold Out His Arms and Fly?" which appeared
    in *Foundation* (July 1973).

LORD DUNSANY (E.J.M.D. PLUNKET, 18th BARON DUNSANY)

250. Amory, Mary. *Biography of Lord Dunsany*. London:
    Collins, 1972. 288pp.

    A biographical study which utilizes Dunsany's
    autobiographies, his letters, and his wife's
    diary. Lacks extensive scholarly apparatus. In-
    cludes a chronological checklist of Dunsany's
    published books. Indexed.

HARLAN ELLISON

251. Slusser, George Edgar. *Harlan Ellison: Unrepentant
    Harlequin*. San Bernardino, CA: Borgo Press,
    1977. 63pp. [paper].

    A literary study of Ellison's fiction and non-
    fiction, with sections on "journalism," "fantasy,"
    and "myth," which lay the groundwork for detailed
    analyses of his most ambitious and provocative
    tales to date: "Adrift Just Off the Isles of Lan-
    gerhans: Latitude 38 54'N, Longitude 77 00'13W,"
    and "The Deathbird." Brief checklist of published
    books.

252. Swigart, Leslie Kay. *Harlan Ellison: A Biblio-
    graphical Checklist*. Dallas: Williams, 1973.
    117pp. [paper].

    A descriptive checklist of Ellison's fiction and
    non-fiction published in English and foreign lan-
    guage books and periodicals through April 1973.
    The material is arranged chronologically in ten
    sections: books written or edited by Ellison, with
    contents, editions, and printings indicated; scripts
    which were produced; fiction, including reprints
    and translations; articles and essays; introductions
    and afterwords; reviews; published letters; publish-
    ed interviews; fanzines edited by Ellison; and

73

titles of books, films, and TV series announced but
unpublished. Includes a long biographical sketch of
Ellison by Swigart as well as comments and appraisals by Isaac Asimov, Ben Bova, Edward Bryant, Joanna Russ, Robert Silverberg, and James Sutherland.
An added feature is the inclusion of numerous photographs of Ellison, book covers, dust jackets,
magazine and comic book covers, etc. The work is
thorough and professional and is a model which
many SF bibliographers would do well to emulate.

PHILIP JOSE FARMER

253. Knapp, Lawrence. *The First Editions of Philip Jose
Farmer*. Menlo Park, CA: David G. Turner, 1976.
8pp. [paper].

A bibliographic checklist with material arranged
in four sections: books, listed in chronological
sequence by year of publication, with collection
contents noted and indication of earlier publication where applicable; uncollected stories arranged alphabetically; articles on Farmer and his
work; and a series listing. The checklist covers
U.S. imprints only.

JOHN RUSSELL FEARN

254. Harbottle, Philip. *The Multi-Man: A Biographic and
Bibliographic Study of John Russell Fearn (1908-
60)*. Wallsend, Northumberland, England: By the
Author, 1968. 69pp. [paper].

To date, the most extensive study of Fearn and his
writings. Based upon two earlier studies by Harbottle, *John Russell Fearn--An Evaluation* (1963)
and *John Russell Fearn: The Ultimate Analysis* (1965).
Comprises a long biographical essay with analysis of
Fearn's writing style and literary output and a complete checklist of his writings in books and periodicals. The annotated checklist is divided into five
parts: science fiction, detective fiction, western
fiction, romantic fiction, and film criticism. Where
applicable these parts are subdivided into fiction
and non-fiction and the listings are chronological
by pseudonym if employed. An exhaustive work which
badly needs an index.

255. Cohen, Morton N. *Rider Haggard: His Life and Works.*
London: Hutchinson, 1960. 327pp. Rpt. New York:
Walker, 1961.

The standard biography. A critical evaluation that
treats all of Haggard's writing: fiction, political,
economic, and social history and commentary. Contains valuable information on influences, sources,
friends, contemporaries, and contemporary appraisals as well as a bibliography of published and
unpublished fiction and non-fiction, reviews of
Haggard's publications, works about him, and the
literary and historical backgrounds of his age.

256. Scott, J.E. *A Bibliography of the Works of Sir
Henry Rider Haggard 1856-1925.* Takeley, Bishop's
Stortford, Herts., England: Elkin Matthews, 1947.
258pp.

Although riddled with bibliographical errors (especially in the ordering of the earliest printing of
the author's novels), this descriptive bibliography
remains the most detailed and comprehensive study
of the published writings by and about Haggard. The
work is arranged chronologically and divided into
nine sections as follows: books; articles in newspapers and periodicals; reports of speeches; reviews; dramatizations; parodies of his works; and
published interviews with Haggard, and biographical
and critical material about him. Researchers are
advised to also consult Donald M. Day's *Bibliography
of Adventure* (see IV A). A new bibliography of Haggard is badly needed.

HARRY HARRISON

257. Biamonti, Francesco. *Harry Harrison: Bibliographia
(1951-1965).* Trieste: Editoriale Libraria,
1965. 11pp. [paper].

An alphabetical checklist with publishing history
of Harrison's fiction and non-fiction writings in
books and periodicals through January 1965. A few
of the entries are briefly annotated by Harrison.

75

ROBERT A. HEINLEIN

258. Owings, Mark. *Robert A. Heinlein: A Bibliography*.
     Baltimore: Croatan House, 1973. 23pp. [paper].

     A checklist of Heinlein's fiction and non-fiction
     published in books and periodicals arranged alpha-
     betically by title. Cites the first appearance as
     well as subsequent printings in English and in
     foreign translation. Title changes are cross-ref-
     erenced and reprint collections are listed. Despite
     the poor layout of information, a comprehensive
     and useful checklist.

259. Panshin, Alexei. *Heinlein in Dimension: A Critical
     Analysis*. Chicago: Advent, 1968. 204pp.

     The only book-length critical analysis of Heinlein's
     writing published to date. The fiction is evaluated
     in terms of its subject matter, plot structure, and
     style. Also discussed are "The Heinlein Individual"
     and Heinlein's influence in the field of science
     fiction. Contains a chronological checklist of U.S.
     appearances of Heinlein's fiction in books and mag-
     azines from 1939 through 1967. Indexed.

260. Searles, Baird. *Stranger in a Strange Land & Other
     Works*. Lincoln, NE: Cliffs Notes, 1975. 59pp.
     [paper].

     A better than average study organized into the fol-
     lowing sections: life of the author, background:
     science fiction in the '30s, the early novels and
     short stories, the adult novels and short stories,
     the juvenile novels, the transitional novels, the
     novels of the '70s, and the Heinlein superstructure
     (which includes the "Future History" framework and
     Heinlein's major themes). Contains a selected check-
     list of Heinlein's fiction, citing titles and dates
     of first publication only; contents of collections
     are listed.

261. Slusser, George Edgar. *Robert A. Heinlein: Stranger
     in His Own Land*. San Bernardino: Borgo Press,
     1976. 60pp. [paper].

     A critical essay charting "Heinlein's development,
     from his days as a pulp and juvenile writer to his
     enshrinement as a hero of the counter-culture."
     Includes a checklist of Heinlein's published books;
     cites first appearance only.

262. Allen, L. David. *Herbert's Dune and Other Works.*
Lincoln, NE: Cliffs Notes, 1975. 101pp.
[paper].

An extensive survey of the following Herbert novels:
*Dune, Dune Messiah, The Godmakers, Under Pressure,
Destination: Void, The Eyes of Heisenberg, The Green
Brain, The Santaroga Barrier, Whipping Star,* and
Hellstrom's Hive.

ROBERT E. HOWARD

263. De Camp, L. Sprague. *The Conan Reader;* De Camp and
George H. Scithers, *The Conan Grimore* and *The
Conan Swordbook.* (See III B2)

264. De Camp, L. Sprague. *The Miscast Barbarian: A Biography of Robert E. Howard (1906-1936).* Saddle
River, NJ: Gerry de la Ree, 1975. 43pp. [paper].

This biographical essay first appeared in an abbrev-
iated version in the June 1971 issue of *Fantastic
Stories.* This enlarged version appears in a reorgan-
ized form as the Howard chapter in De Camp's *Literary Swordsmen and Sorcerers* (see III B2).

265. Falconer, Lee N. *A gazeteer of the Hyborian World
of Conan, Including Also the World of Kull and
an Ethnogeographical Dictionary of the Principal
Peoples of the Era.* West Linn, OR: Starmont
House, 1977. 119pp. [paper].

A compilation of more than 450 entries, plus appendices, which clarify the place names, nations, and
peoples of Howard's imaginary world. Although complete in itself, this work was intended as a companion to the Starmont map of the Hyborian World. Published here for the first time are Howard's own
background notes on various peoples of the Hyborian
age.

266. Lord, Glenn. *The Last Celt: A Bio-bibliography of
Robert Ervin Howard.* West Kingston, RI: Donald M.
Grant, 1976. 416pp.

To date the most important reference tool for the
study of the life and writings of Howard. Material
for biographical study includes five autobiographical

pieces written by Howard over a lapse of years and
five biographical sketches and reminiscences by
Alvin Earl Perry, H.P. Lovecraft, Glenn Lord, E.
Hoffmann Price, and Harold Preece. The comprehensive
descriptive bibliography is organized alphabetically
by title and under pseudonyms where applicable, with
the exception of the listing of published books
which is arranged in chronological sequence. The
listing is divided as follows: published books (with
coverage through 1973) incorporating full bibliographical citation and reprint information where applicable; checklist of fiction (story title changes are
noted and are cross-referenced); verse (including
first line and heading indices); articles and other
non-fiction prose writings; published letters (alphabetically arranged by addressee); writings indexed alphabetically by periodical; translations;
unpublished fiction, verse, and articles; series
index; lost manuscripts; unborn books; comics; television adaptation; list of extant copies of *The Jun-
to*; books and periodical articles about Howard and
his writings; and Conan pastiches. The concluding
"miscellanea" includes texts of unpublished REH material, facsimiles of letters, a fanzine, map, illustrations of pulp covers, etc.

267. Weinberg, Robert. *The Annotated Guide to Robert E.
Howard's Sword & Sorcery*. West Linn, OR: Starmont House, 1976. 152pp. [paper].

Plot summaries of the sword-and-sorcery fiction
with critical commentary on the fiction and Howard's
writing in general.

ALDOUS HUXLEY

268. Eschelbach, Claire John and Joyce Lee Shober.
Aldous Huxley: A Bibliography, 1916-1959.
Berkeley: University of California Press, 1961.
150pp.

A checklist of Huxley's writings, including foreign
translations, arranged as follows: writings of Huxley (books and pamphlets; articles; essays and
short stories; adaptations) and works about Huxley
(bibliography; books and pamphlets; dissertations;
essays in books; periodical articles; criticism of
individual works). Index of names. Continued by
Thomas D. Clareson and Carolyn S. Andrews, "Aldous
Huxley: A Bibliography 1960-1964," (*Extrapolation*,
December 1964).

269. Kuehn, Robert E., ed. *Aldous Huxley: A Collection of Critical Essays*. Englewood Cliffs, NJ: Prentice-Hall, 1974. 188pp.

Twelve essays evaluate the radical departure from traditional forms in Huxley's works. Most of the essays have been published since the author's death. Only one essay *per se* deals with Huxley's science fiction work, "Vision and Symbol in Aldous Huxley's *Island*" by Donald J. Watt.

270. Watt, Donald, ed. *Aldous Huxley: The Critical Heritage*. London: Routledge & Kegan Paul, 1975. 493pp.

A collection of major reviews of Huxley's writings during the period 1918 to 1965. The reviews are arranged chronologically according to the date of publication of the titles reviewed, and include sections on *Brave New World* and *Island*.

URSULA K. LE GUIN

271. Le Guin, Ursula K. *Dreams Must Explain Themselves*. New York: Algol Press, 1975. 37pp. [paper].

Contains an essay, "Dreams Must Explain Themselves," which discusses the Earthsea trilogy and its genesis; "The Rule of Names," an early fantasy story which contains details of setting for the Earthsea novels; the 1972 National Book Award acceptance speech; and an interview in which Le Guin makes some important comments despite the ineptness of the interviewer.

272. Slusser, George Edgar. *The Farthest Shores of Ursula K. Le Guin*. San Bernardino, CA: Borgo Press, 1976. 60pp. [paper].

A study of the growing complexity of Le Guin's themes, settings, and characters as they develop in the Hanish novels, *The Left Hand of Darkness,* the Earthsea trilogy, and *The Dispossessed*. Focuses on Le Guin's moralistic theme, the nature of human evil. Contains a primary bibliography of Le Guin's stories and novels.

CLIVE STAPLES LEWIS

273. Christopher, Joe R. and Joan K. Ostling. *C.S. Lewis: An Annotated Checklist of Writings about him and his Works*. [Kent, OH]: Kent State University Press, 1973. 389pp.

This comprehensive checklist annotates all the important secondary material about Lewis and his writings, from selected reviews of his books and periodical articles to book-length studies and graduate research. Material is arranged into the following categories: general and unclassifiable items; biographical essays, personality sketches, and news items; fiction and poetry; religion and ethics; literary criticism; selected book reviews; books and pamphlets about Lewis. Indices include a listing of Masters' Theses and Doctoral Dissertations. Indexed by author and title.

274. Gibb, Jocelyn, ed. *Light on C.S. Lewis*. London: Geoffrey Bles, 1965. 160pp.

A collection of essays by people who knew him written shortly after Lewis' death. Contains a comprehensive checklist of Lewis' books and periodical contributions, arranged chronologically into seven sections: books, short stories, books edited or with prefaces by Lewis, essays and pamphlets, poems, book reviews, and published letters.

275. Green, Roger Lancelyn and Walter Hooper. *C.S. Lewis: A Biography*. London: Collins, 1974. 320pp.

The authorized biography, written by two of his friends, supervised by Lewis' brother, Warren Hamilton Lewis, and composed with full access to family papers and to Lewis' diaries, letters, and manuscripts. In addition to biographical detail, the study analyzes the influences which shaped his intellectual life. Green and Hooper stress that this work be supplemented with Lewis' autobiographical effort, *Surprised by Joy: The Shape of My Early Life* and by *Letters of C.S. Lewis,* ed. Warren Lewis.

DAVID LINDSAY

276. Pick, J.B., Colin Wilson, and E.H. Visiak. *The Strange Genius of David Lindsay*. London: John Baker, 1970. 183pp.

To date, the only book on Lindsay. Includes a thirty
page biography and literary appraisal by Pick, followed by essays by Wilson, Visiak and Pick. Wilson's
essay, "Lindsay As Novelist and Mystic," is a perceptive analysis of *A Voyage to Arcturus,* a work
which he considers to be "one of the greatest novels
of the twentieth century, and arguably *the* greatest
work of imaginative fiction of our time." Visiak, a
long time friend of Lindsay, provides biographical
data as well as an analysis of *The Haunted Woman*
and *Devil's Tor.* His comments on *Arcturus* are of
special interest. Pick provides a study of *The Vio-
let Apple* and *The Witch,* two novels then unpublished
(both are now available in a single volume edited by
Pick, with an introduction by Wilson, as *The Violent
Apple & The Witch,* Chicago: Chicago Review Press,
1976).

JACK LONDON

277. Walker, Dale L. *The Alien Worlds of Jack London.*
Grand Rapids, MI: Wolf House Books, 1973. 47pp.
[paper].

A critical study and chronological checklist of
London's fantasy titles.

278. Walker, Dale L. and James E. Sisson III. *The Fiction
of Jack London: A Chronological Bibliography.*
El Paso: Texas Western Press, 1972. 40pp.

An annotated checklist, with information on sources
and reprints as well as critical commentary, of
London's fiction.

279. Woodbridge, Hensley C., John London and George H.
Tweney. *Jack London: A Bibliography.* Georgetown,
CA: Talisman Press, 1966. 385pp. Enl. ed. Mil-
wood, NY: Kraus Reprint, 1973. 554pp.

The most comprehensive bibliography of writings by
and about London in English and foreign language
books and periodicals. First editions are listed
with full descriptive bibliographic citations, while
other material is recorded in checklist format with
contents listing and notes where applicable. The
1973 editions contains extensive additions to the
original edition as well as new material published
in the interim and compiled solely by Woodbridge.

HOWARD PHILLIPS LOVECRAFT

280. Carter, Lin. *Lovecraft: A Look Behind the "Cthulhu Mythos."* New York: Ballantine Books, 1972. 198pp. [paper].

A study of the growth of the Cthulhu Mythos in the fiction of Lovecraft and others who adopted it or developed it in their own writings. The focus is upon Lovecraft's life and philosophy and its influence on his writings. Includes an extensive checklist of the mythos which corrects errors and omissions in previous checklists by Robert E. Briney (1955), Jack L. Chalker (1966), and Robert E. Weinberg (1969). *Reader's Guide to the Cthulhu Mythos* by Robert E. Weinberg and E.P. Berglund (1973) is now the more extensive checklist (see III B2).

281. Cook, W. Paul. *In Memoriam Howard Phillips Lovecraft: Recollections, Appreciations, Estimates.* n.p.: Driftwood Press, 1941. 76pp. [paper]. Rpt. *H.P. Lovecraft: A Portrait.* Baltimore: Mirage Press, 1968. 66pp. [paper].

The first substantial memoir of Lovecraft, written by a close friend and publisher of his first book. This memoir was reprinted in *Beyond the Wall of Sleep* (1943), the second major collection of Lovecraft's fiction, as "H.P. Lovecraft: An Appreciation." It was reissued separately in 1968 with a note on Cook by Jack L. Chalker.

282. De Camp, L. Sprague. *Lovecraft: A Biography.* Garden City: Doubleday, 1975. 510pp.

The first full-length, and to date the most comprehensive, biography of Lovecraft. The appraisals and conclusions provided by de Camp in this well documented historical and analytical biography have generated much controversy within the circle of Lovecraft devotees. Extensive checklist of primary and secondary sources. Indexed.

283. Derleth, August. *H.P.L.: A Memoir.* New York: Ben Abramson, 1945. 123pp.

A personal view of Lovecraft and his writings by his literary executor and chief publicist. Lovecraft's writings are widely known today largely as a result of Derleth's efforts.

284. Derleth, August. *Some Notes on H.P. Lovecraft.*
Sauk City, WI: Arkham House, 1959. 62pp. [paper].
Rpt. Folcroft, PA: Folcroft Press, 1974.

Examines various "myths" concerning Lovecraft's life
and writings. Of interest are Derleth's comments on
Lovecraft's manuscript fragments and notes (he left
no uncompleted stories) and his use of them for col-
laborations and for his own tales. Also prints R.H.
Barlow's notes concerning Lovecraft's 1934 visit to
Florida and the texts of four letters from HPL to
Derleth.

285. Grant, Donald M. and Thomas P. Hadley, eds. *Rhode
Island on Lovecraft.* Providence, RI: Grant-Hadley,
1945. 26pp. [paper].

Includes reminiscences of Lovecraft by Mrs. Clifford
Eddy, Marian F. Barner, and Mary V. Dana, and essays
by Dorothy C. Walter and Winfield Townley Scott.

286. Long, Frank Belknap. *Howard Phillips Lovecraft:
Dreamer on the Nightside.* Sauk City, WI: Arkham
House, 1975. 237pp.

A very personal biographical memoir by a former
close friend and member of the original Lovecraft
circle. Much of the narrative is set forth in dialogue form and the work lacks all scholarly apparatus. Aside from a few biographical details, Long
presents little that is new or interesting, and the
book is tedious reading. The biography by de Camp
is the recommended life.

287. Lovecraft, Howard Phillips. *Autobiography: Some
Notes on a Nonentity.* Sauk City, WI: Arkham
House, 1963. 17pp. [paper].

An autobiographical statement of approximately 2000
words written November 23, 1933; annotated by August
Derleth. This document was first published (accord-
to Owings and Chalker) in *Boy's Hearld*, October 1941.
Collected in Lovecraft's *Beyond the Wall of Sleep*
(1943).

288. Lovecraft, Howard Phillips. *Ec'h--Pi--El Speaks: An
Autobiographical Sketch by H.P. Lovecraft.*
Saddle River, NJ: Gerry de la Ree, 1972. 12pp.
[paper].

A sketch of approximately 3000 words written in July
1929. De la Ree does not provide a source for this
document, but it appears to be all (or a portion)
of a letter.

289. Lovecraft, Howard Phillips. *Selected Letters*. 5 vols.
     Sauk City, WI: Arkham House, 1965-76.

     Collects 930 letters written between 1911 and 1937.
     Volumes 1-3 are edited by August Derleth and Donald
     Wandrei; volumes 4-5 are edited by Derleth and James
     Turner. The letters are arranged in chronological
     order by date and the table of contents listing pro-
     vides a synopsis of each. Not indexed.

290. Lovecraft, Howard Phillips and Willis Conover.
     Lovecraft at Last. Arlington, VA: Carrollton,
     Clark, 1975. 272pp.

     A moving chronicle of the eight-month (July 1936-
     March 1937) correspondence between fifteen-year old
     Conover and forty-six-year old Lovecraft which ter-
     minated at the latter's death. These letters and
     Conover's connective text are arranged to form a
     highly effective narrative. The physical layout of
     the book is impressive, with skillful rendering of
     the extensive facsimile work. A calendar of Love-
     craft's letters to Conover is included. Indexed.

291. Owings, Mark and Irving Binkin. *A Catalog of Love-
     craftiana: The Grill/Binkin Collection*. Baltimore:
     Mirage Press, 1975. 71pp.

     A valuable listing, comprising an illustrated check-
     list of 668 entries, of what is certainly one of
     the most important privately owned Lovecraft col-
     lections. Of importance are the brief annotations
     of the contents of the Lovecraft manuscripts and
     letters.

292. Owings, Mark with Jack L. Chalker. *The Revised H.P.
     Lovecraft Bibliography*. Baltimore: Mirage Press,
     1973. 43pp. [paper].

     The most comprehensive checklist of writings by and
     about Lovecraft in English and foreign language
     books and professional and amateur magazines. The
     compilers note that "in 90% of the cases, we have
     seen and examined the actual items herein." It is
     regretable that the unexamined material was not so
     indicated. The checklist is arranged alphabetically
     in eight sections: essays, verse, fiction, collect-
     ions, revisions, mythos stories, comic book adapta-
     tions, and material on Lovecraft. Full printing his-
     tory for each entry is provided and any subsequent
     appearance in periodicals, anthologies, and collect-
     ed editions of Lovecraft's work is indicated. While
     books collecting Lovecraft's writings are listed
     separately, there is no section providing a complete

listing of all his books and pamphlet publications; thus to identify his pamphlet *Looking Backwards*, one must consult the "essays" section, where it is listed following the initial periodical appearance. Therefore, Chalker's "Howard Phillips Lovecraft: A Bibliography," in *The Dark Brotherhood and Other Pieces by H.P. Lovecraft and Divers Hands* (Sauk City: Arkham House, 1966), is to be preferred for the identification of books and pamphlets by and about Lovecraft. It is hoped that Owings and Chalker will adopt this latter format if they contemplate future revision of their Lovecraft checklist.

293. Schweitzer, Darrell, ed. *Essays Lovecraftian*. Baltimore: T-K Graphics, 1976. 114pp. [paper].

Essays on Lovecraft and his writings, some of which appear for the first time while others are collected primarily from amateur magazines, including *Nyctalops* and *Whispers*. Among the fifteen essays are a few which stand out as significant contributions to Lovecraft scholarship. Of special interest are "The Four Faces of the Outsider" by Dirk W. Mosig and "Lovecraft and Lord Dunsany" by Darrell Schweitzer.

294. Shreffler, Philip A. *The H.P. Lovecraft Companion*. Westport, CT: Greenwood Press, 1977. 199pp.

Analysis of and concordance to Lovecraft's weird fiction. Divided into four sections: the first comprises a long introductory essay providing a critical analysis which traces the literary influences on Lovecraft's work as well as the effect of his work on his literary successors. The second, and most extensive, section summarizes each of his 62 major stories with fourteen of them subjected to extended discussion of their geographical, biographical, and literary sources. Section three provides a concordance of named fictional characters and monsters in the stories, as well as many of the historical non-fiction individuals who figure in works. The last section is an examination of Lovecraft's "Mythos" entities. Appendices describe the Hermetic Order of the Golden Dawn and print Lovecraft's "The History and Chronology of the *Necronomicon*." Briefly annotated checklist of primary and secondary material. Indexed.

295. Wetzel, George, ed. *The Lovecraft Collectors Library, Volume VI. Commentaries*. North Tonawanda, NY: SSR Publications, 1955. 37pp. [paper].

Two memoirs of Lovecraft, two essays on his fiction,
and a comment on his eccentricities collected from
amateur magazines. This material was also collected
in *Howard Phillips Lovecraft: Memoirs, Critiques &
Bibliographies* (North Tonawanda: SSR Publications,
1955). This latter compilation was, according to the
publisher, simultaneously issued with volumes six
and seven of *The Lovecraft Collectors Library*. It
contains some material not present in either volume.
Though now out of date, *The Lovecraft Collectors
Library, Volume VII. Bibliographies* (North Tonawanda, SSR Publications, 1955), compiled by George
Wetzel and Robert E. Briney, was the first comprehensive Lovecraft checklist and remained the standard bibliography until the 1962 Chalker version.

GEORGE MACDONALD

296. MacDonald, Greville. *George MacDonald and his Wife.*
London: Allen & Unwin, 1924. 575pp.

The standard, if biased, biography. Should be sup-
plemented by Greville MacDonald, *Reminiscences of
a Specialist* (Unwin & Allen, 1932) and Roderick F.
McGillis, "The Fantastic Imagination: The Prose
Romances of George MacDonald," Ph.D. dissertation,
University of Reading, 1973.

297. Reis, Richard H. *George MacDonald.* New York:
Twayne Publishers, 1972. 161pp.

A critical-analytical study of MacDonald's place in
literature. Examines all aspects of his career, including his life, his central philosophical ideas,
and the nature of symbolism and its effects upon
MacDonald's work. Includes a chronology of MacDonald's life and a selected bibliography of his novels,
short stories, essays, sermons, and criticism. Also
included is a brief annotated list of secondary
sources.

298. Wolff, Robert Lee. *The Golden Key: A Study of the
Fiction of George MacDonald.* New Haven: Yale
University Press, 1961. 425pp.

A Freudian study of MacDonald's fiction which approaches his work as symptomatic of his neuroses.
Also contains a careful and thorough tracing of
influences upon MacDonald's work, especially by
the German Romantics.

ARTHUR MACHEN

299. Goldstone, Adrian and Wesley Sweetser. *A Bibli-*
     ography of Arthur Machen. Austin: University
     of Texas, 1965. 180pp.

The most comprehensive bibliography of the published
writings of Machen in books, pamphlets, periodicals,
and newspapers. Chronological listing in the following divisions: books and pamphlets (full descriptive
citations of first editions with reprints and new
editions noted when issued); translations; contributions to books; and magazine and newspaper contributions. While selective, the final section of
works of criticism and commentary on Machen in books
and periodicals is extensive. Indexed.

300. Starrett, Vincent. *Arthur Machen: A Novelist of*
     Ecstasy and Sin. Chicago: Walter M. Hill, 1918.
     35pp.

The first book-length study of Machen by a journal-
ist/critic who was an early champion of his writing
and whose efforts brought Machen to the attention
of the American reading public. For an account of
their literary relationship see Vincent Starrett
and Arthur Machen, *Starrett vs. Machen: A Record*
of Discovery and Correspondence (St. Louis: Auto-
lycus Press, 1977).

ABRAHAM MERRITT

301. Wentz, Walter J. *A. Merritt: A Bibliography of*
     Fantastic Writings. Roseville, CA: George A.
     Bibby, 1965. 33pp. [paper].

The most comprehensive checklist of Merritt's fantasy and science fiction published in books and
periodicals. The awkward format is somewhat offset
by the extensive and valuable annotations and commentary.

MICHAEL MOORCOCK

302. Harper, Andrew and George McAulay. *Michael Moorcock:*
     A Bibliography. Baltimore: T-K Graphics, 1976.
     29pp. [paper].

An incomplete and inaccurate checklist of Moorcock's books. Not comprehensive; misleading. Researchers should avoid it.

ST. THOMAS MORE

303. Gibson, R.W. *St. Thomas More: A Preliminary Bibliography of his Works and Moreana to the Year 1750. . . With a Bibliography of Utopiana Compiled by R.W. Gibson and J. Max Patrick.* New Haven: Yale University Press, 1961. 499pp.

To date the most comprehensive analytical and descriptive bibliography of More's works and works about him to 1750. Additionally, there are 442 entries of Moreana published to 1750. Germane to this study is section IX, which lists, with extensive annotations, 190 utopian and dystopian works published from 1500 to 1750. In addition, this section includes: a short-title list of some bibliographies and books about utopias and related literatures; and some references to More and his *Utopia*, the word "utopia," and the genre, 1500-1700. Section X is a listing of eighteen utopian addresses. Additional titles are noted and some are briefly discussed in the introduction to section IX. An essential reference for the study of utopian and dystopian fiction to 1750. Extensive index.

TALBOT MUNDY

304. Day, Bradford M. *Talbot Mundy Biblio. Materials Toward a Bibliography of the Works of Talbot Mundy.* New York: Science-Fiction & Fantasy Publications, 1955. 28pp. [paper].

A checklist of books and magazine fiction by Mundy. Includes a brief biographical sketch by Day and a five-page article and checklist on Mundy's sagas and series by Dr. J. Lloyd Eaton. Collected in Day's *Bibliography of Adventure* (see IV A) in a revised version.

ANDRE NORTON (ALICE MARY NORTON)

305. Turner, David G. *The First Editions of Andre Norton.* Menlo Park, CA: David G. Turner, 1974. 12pp. [paper].

A chronological checklist of Norton's books, magazine fiction, anthology appearances, and a non-
fiction article. A useful guide, but misses a few
contributions to books, some of which can be located
in the checklist in *The Many Worlds of Andre Norton*,
ed. Roger Elwood (Chilton Books, 1974).

GEORGE ORWELL (ERIC ARTHUR BLAIR)

306. Small, Christopher. *The Road to Miniluv: George
     Orwell, the State, and God*. London: Victor
     Gollancz, 1975. 220pp. Rpt. Pittsburgh: Univer-
     sity of Pittsburgh Press, 1976.

The author shows, in a fascinating analysis of
Orwell's early novels, how close are the links
between his life, his obsessions, and his crea-
tions. Followed by a penetrating examination of
Animal Farm and *1984*.

307. Steinhoff, William. *George Orwell and the Origins
     of 1984*. Ann Arbor: University of Michigan
     Press, 1975. 288pp.

A study of *1984* as the culminating expression of
Orwell's ideas and artistry, with a thorough account of the experiences and intellectual context
from which the novel emerged. Analyzes the major
themes of *1984* and shows how they were shaped by
Orwell's reading and the era in which he lived.
The analysis includes a discussion of the precur-
sors to *1984* and the nature of utopia and totali-
tarianism. Steinhoff traces themes in Orwell's
earlier novels, particularly regarding intellectuals
and their relation to society, and shows how they
are represented in *1984*. The study concludes with
observations on the social and political significance of the novel. Heavy documentation. Extensive
primary and secondary bibliography. Indexed.

308. Williams, Raymond, ed. *George Orwell: A Collection
     of Critical Essays*. Englewood Cliffs, NJ:
     Prentice-Hall, 1974. 182pp.

The essays are arranged in an order that in general
follows the chronology of Orwell's literary development. Strikes an even balance in considering his
total output. While most of the essays contain references to *1984*, only three bear directly upon it:
"Orwell as a Satirist" by Stephen J. Greenblatt,
"*1984*--The Mysticism of Cruelty" by Isaac Deutscher,
and "Orwell's Post-War Prophecy" by Jenni Calder.

309. Batchelor, John. *Mervyn Peake: A Biographical and Critical Exploration*. London: Duckworth, 1976. 176pp.

Using personal reminiscences and published and un-published sources, Batchelor furnishes a biography and the first extended literary study of Peake, with emphasis on an analysis of the Titus novels: *Titus Groan, Gormenghast, Titus Alone* (inaccurately refer-red to as the "Gormenghast Trilogy"). Peake's un-successful novel, *Mr. Pye*, is also discussed along with his shorter fiction and poetry. The bibliogra-phy lists primary material (both published and un-published) and selected references. Indexed.

310. Metzger, Arthur. *A Guide to the Gormenghast Trilogy*. Baltimore: T-K Graphics, 1976. 35pp. [paper].

A concordance to people and places named in Peake's Titus novels. The introduction by Michael Moorcock is adapted from his obituary published in *New Worlds* (February 1969).

311. Watney, John. *Mervyn Peake*. London: Michael Joseph, 1976. 255pp.

To date the most comprehensive biography, written by a long-time friend of the Peakes. Compiled from interviews, correspondence, and fragments of infor-mation collected over a five-year period with the full co-operation of Maeve Peake. This is not a critical study, though some analysis of Peake's art and writing is provided. Batchelor is the preferred study.

EDGAR ALLAN POE

312. Heartman, Charles F. and James R. Canney. *A Bibli-ography of First Printings of the Writings of Edgar Allan Poe. Together With a Record of First and Contemporary Later Printings of his Contri-butions to Annuals, Anthologies, Periodicals, and Newspapers Issued During his Lifetime. Also Some Spurious Poeana and Fakes*. rev. ed. Hattiesburg, MS: Book Farm, 1943. 294pp.

Although not free of error, this revised edition of
the 1940 edition remains the most recent and the
most comprehensive descriptive bibliography of first
printings of Poe's writings and later printings issued during his lifetime. Students of Poe should also
consult the following: J. Lasley Dameron, *Edgar Allan
Poe: A Checklist of Criticism 1942-1960* (Charlottesville, 1966); Jay B. Hubbell, "Poe," in *Eight American Authors*, ed. Floyd Stoval (New York, 1956),
rev. ed. with supplement ed. J. Chesley Matthews
(New York, 1963); and John W. Robertson, *A Bibliography of the Writings of Edgar A. Poe* (San Francisco, 1934). A very selective listing of the more
recent essays and books touching upon Poe is Robert
D. Jacobs, "Edgar Allan Poe (1809-1849)," in *A Bibliographical Guide To the Study of Southern Literature*, ed. Louis D. Rubin, Jr. (Baton Rouge, 1969).

SAX ROHMER (ARTHUR SARSFIELD WARD)

313. Ash, Cay Van and Elizabeth Sax Rohmer. *Master of
     Villainy: A Biography of Sax Rohmer*. Ed. Robert
     E. Briney. Bowling Green, OH: Bowling Green
     University Popular Press, 1972. 312pp.

The only book-length account of Rohmer's life and
writings. Originally intended as a collaboration
by Rohmer and his wife, the book remained unfinished
at the time of his death. The project was continued
by Mrs. Rohmer and Ash, a friend and protege of her
husband. The resultant manuscript was not a formal
biography, but a collection of reminiscences and
anecdotes with emphasis on people and events with
dates and chronology often obscure. Briney's bibliographical data provided the structure in which
the material developed by Mrs. Rohmer and Ash was
placed. His annotations have been incorporated into
the text or follow the biography. The chronological
checklist of Rohmer's books and listing of characters and series supersedes that of Day in *Bibliography of Adventure* (see IV A). Indexed.

314. Day, Bradford M. *Sax Rohmer: A Bibliography*. Denver,
     NY: Science-Fiction & Fantasy Publications,
     1963. 34pp. [paper].

Contains a short biographical sketch and a checklist
of Rohmer's books and magazine fiction. The checklist has some inaccurate information and the citations are often incomplete. A revised version appears
in Day's *Bibliography of Adventure* (see IV A). Still

of some use for the magazine fiction, but Robert E.
Briney's checklist in Van Ash and Rohmer, *Master of
Villainy* (which see) should be consulted for a list-
ing of Rohmer's books.

JAMES H. SCHMITZ

315. Owings, Mark. *James H. Schmitz: A Bibliography*.
Baltimore: Croatan House, 1973. 33pp. [paper].

A checklist of Schmitz's fiction in books and professional magazines listed alphabetically by title
with additional separate listings of books (alphabetically) and magazines (chronologically). A
slight work preceded by an introductory essay by
Janet Kagan which provides an overzealous defense
of Schmitz's male chauvinism.

MARY WOLLSTONECRAFT SHELLEY

316. Lyles, W.H. *Mary Shelley: An Annotated Bibliography*.
New York: Garland Publishing, 1975. 297pp.

To date the most comprehensive checklist of writings
by and about Shelley. In addition to books written
or edited by her, contributions to books and periodicals are also listed. The checklist of secondary
material includes items about or relating to her
writings in books, portions of books, periodical
articles, reviews, and graduate research in English
and foreign language publications. Appendices include her works chronologically arranged; a recount-
ing of the legend of George Frankenstein; theatrical,
film and television versions of *Frankenstein*; and
selling prices for selected works by and about Shelley. Extensive index.

317. Small, Christopher. *Ariel Like a Harpy: Shelley,
Mary and* Frankenstein. London: Victor Gollancz,
1972. 352pp. Rpt. *Mary Shelley's Frankenstein:
Tracing the Myth*. Pittsburgh: University of
Pittsburgh Press, 1973.

Shelley's background is explored in depth in an
attempt to outline the factors which caused her to
write *Frankenstein*. The novel is analyzed against
the promise of the machine, "its monstrous effects
in the enslavement of men to industry, their trans-
formation into machines themselves."

318. Tropp, Martin. *Mary Shelley's Monster*. Boston:
     Houghton Mifflin, 1976. 192pp.

     A study of the origins of *Frankenstein* which traces
     the relationships of the characters and themes to
     Shelley's life. Discusses the figures of the Mad
     Scientist and the Monster and how they have permea-
     ted science fiction literature and films. Contains
     a selected chronology of Frankenstein films, 1910-
     1974, and an extensive bibliography of further read-
     ing divided into the following categories: works by
     Shelley; biographies of Shelley, criticism of *Frank-
     enstein*; criticism of plays, films, and literature
     influenced by *Frankenstein*; and related materials.
     Indexed.

319. Walling, William A. *Mary Shelley*. New York: Twayne
     Publishers, 1972. 173pp.

     A fine critical biography which evaluates Shelley's
     mertis and deficiencies as a writer in terms of her
     total output of novels, stories, biographies, tra-
     velogues, letters, journals, and verse. Walling con-
     cludes that her reputation as a minor figure in
     English literature is deserved.

                    MATTHEW PHIPPS SHIEL

320. Morse, A. Reynolds. *The Works of M.P. Shiel: A Study
     in Bibliography*. Los Angeles: Fantasy Publishing
     Company, 1948. 170pp.

     The most comprehensive bibliography to date of the
     published and unpublished writings of Shiel. This
     volume collates or lists all known editions of
     Shiel's books and pamphlets, including translations
     and collaborations. It includes checklists of short
     stories, essays, introductions, articles, transla-
     tions, published letters, etc. appearing in books
     not authored by Shiel, anthologies, periodicals,
     and newspapers. Lists all known manuscripts, cor-
     rected texts, proofs, typescripts, both published
     and unpublished. Writings about Shiel and his works,
     including reviews, in books, magazines, and news-
     papers are recorded. Additional material includes:
     a revised version of Shiel's autobiography, "About
     Myself"; biographical notes by Morse; a description
     and a partial checklist of Shiel's personal library;
     and Edward Shank's funeral address. Morse's book is
     more than a bibliography; in addition to supplying

extensive and valuable historical and descriptive commentary, he provides description and analysis of literary content. Partially indexed.

CLIFFORD D. SIMAK

321. Owings, Mark. *The Electric Bibliograph, Part 1: Clifford D. Simak*. Baltimore: Alice & Jay Haldeman, 1971. [unpaged]. [paper].

A checklist of fiction by Simak, listing original appearances, reprints, title changes, and foreign editions (full publishing data not included for all editions). Not examined. Entry based on listing in Briney and Wood, *SF Bibliographies* (1972). See I B.

CLARK ASHTON SMITH

322. Chalker, Jack L., ed. *In Memoriam Clark Ashton Smith*. Baltimore: Anthem, 1963. 98pp. [paper].

To date the only collection of biographical material on Smith in book form. Introduction by Ray Bradbury and essays and memoirs by Theodore Sturgeon, Donald Fryer, L. Sprague de Camp, Fritz Leiber, and others. Includes an "Autobiography" and other contributions by Smith.

323. Cockcroft, Thomas G.L. *The Tales of Clark Ashton Smith: A Bibliography*. Melling, Lower Hutt, New Zealand: Thomas G.L. Cockcroft, 1951. 5pp. [paper].

Alphabetical checklist of the fiction of Smith, including both original and reprint editions, with separate lists of collections and anthology appearances. A leaf of addenda was published in 1959.

324. Sidney-Fryer, Donald. *The Last of the Great Romantic Poets*. Albuquerque: Silver Scarab Press, 1973. 28pp [paper].

A long critical essay which "is in large part an attempt to define the over-all romance tradition from its beginnings in the Middle Ages on into our own time, and to demonstrate how Smith's own *oeuvre* occupies the principal place in that same tradition for the twentieth century. . . . Similar to the cycles of tales and legends revolving around King

Arthur and Charlemagne, about half of Smith's prose
fictions are cycles of tales laid in such imaginary
worlds as Hyperborea, Atlantis, Averoigne, Zothique,
Xiccarph, and other places. Not only these, but most
of his short stories have the same general tone,
character, and fictional ambiance of the original
metrical romances. These short fictions represent
the most serious and successful attempt to adjust
the great tradition of romantic story-telling to the
twentieth-century sensibility." [Author's "Caveat
Lector."]

CORDWAINER SMITH (PAUL M.A. LINEBARGER)

325. [Porter, Andrew, ed.] *Exploring Cordwainer Smith*.
New York: Algol Press, 1975. 33pp. [paper].

This pamphlet collects a biographical article about
Linebarger, who wrote science fiction under the pen
name Cordwainer Smith, by Arthur Burns; an essay on
the fiction by John Foyster; a conversation between
Burns and Foyster discussing Linebarger and his fiction; and articles by Sandra Miesel (on St. Joan and
the 'D'Joan of "The Dead Lady of Clown Town") and
Alice K. Turner (on the internal chronology of the
Cordwainer Smith stories). Also includes a brief
checklist of published books and magazine fiction.

EDWARD ELMER SMITH

326. Ellik, Ronald and William Evans. *The Universes of
E.E. Smith*. Chicago: Advent, 1966. 272pp.

A concordance to the major writings, the Lensman
series and the Skylark series. Includes a checklist
of Smith's writings compiled by Al Lewis which provides data on the first and later printings in books
and magazines, as well as non-fiction writings on
Smith.

BRAM STOKER (ABRAHAM STOKER)

327. Farson, Daniel. *The Man Who Wrote Dracula: A Biography of Bram Stoker*. London: Michael Joseph,
1975. 240pp. Rpt. New York: St. Martin's Press,
1976.

The most recent biographical study of Stoker, written
by his grandnephew, which for the facts of the life,
draws heavily on Harry Ludlam's earlier work (which
see). There is some analysis of Stoker's writing
with emphasis on *Dracula* and other weird fiction
(as well as a summary of the Dracula legend and
vampire fiction), but it is more of a psychological
examination than a literary one. Farson, who admits
to a total lack of expertise in this area (p. 211),
debunks the Freudian interpretations of *Dracula* by
Dr. Joseph S. Bierman, Professor Royce MacGillivray,
and psychiatrist Seymour Schuster, and lays a case
for the creation of "one of the most erotic books
in English literature" as a subconscious reaction to
his wife's probable frigidity. The book suffers from
lack of coherence in thematic development and structure and, like its predecessor, this biography lacks
satisfactory references. The man who wrote *Dracula*
is still in need of a well-documented biography.

328. Ludlam, Harry. *A Biography of Dracula: The Life
     Story of Bram Stoker*. London: Fireside Press,
     1962. 200pp.

The pioneer biography of Stoker resulting from seven
years of research and access to the family's private
letters, diaries, and photographs. The obligatory
material on *Dracula* is presented along with synopses
of Stoker's other writings, but Ludlam is at his
best when dealing with Stoker's professional connec-
tion with the British stage (as manager of Sir Henry
Irving and the Lyceum) and presenting the history of
Dracula as a play and later in films. No textual
references or sources are provided.

JAMES TIPTREE, JR. (ALICE SHELDON)

329. Dozois, Gardner. *The Fiction of James Tiptree, Jr.*
     New York: Algol Press, 1977. 36pp. [paper].

Reprints a long critical essay on Tiptree's fiction
which appeared originally as the introduction to the
Gregg Press edition of *10,000 Light Years from Home*.
This pamphlet reveals that James Tiptree, Jr. is
Alice Sheldon, a 61-year old semi-retired exterimen-
tal psychologist. Includes a checklist of Alice
Sheldon's writings as James Tiptree, Jr., Raccoona
Sheldon, and Alice Bradley, compiled by Jeffrey
Smith.

JOHN RONALD REUEL TOLKIEN

Note: This section lists selected book-length biographies, critical studies, concordances, and other material published after 1969. For earlier writings on Tolkien and his work consult Richard C. West, *Tolkien Criticism: An Annotated Checklist* (which see).

330. Carpenter, Humphrey. *Tolkien: A Biography*. Boston: Houghton Mifflin, 1977. 287pp.

Carpenter states in his "author's note" that this is "the first published biography" of Tolkien. He is in error, for Daniel Grotta-Kurska's book-length life (which see) was published a full year before Carpenter's study. Tolkien disliked the use of biography as a form of literary criticism and once wrote: "One of my strongest opinions is that investigation of an author's biography is an entirely vain and false approach to his works." Tolkien termed the first published full-length biographical/critical study (William Ready, *The Tolkien Relation*, Chicago, 1968) to be "insulting and offensive" and its appearance destroyed their friendship. Carpenter has endeavored to respect Tolkien's viewpoint and, while he has analyzed some of the literary and other influences that came to bear on Tolkien's imagination as reflected in his fiction, his emphasis is upon a chronological biographical study authorized by Tolkien's children and based upon letters, diaries, and other papers of Tolkien, and upon reminiscences of his family and friends. At present the only source of much biographical data, but Grotta-Kurska's life should also be consulted.

331. Evans, Robley. *J.R.R. Tolkien*. New York: Warner Paperback Library, 1973. 206pp. [paper]. Rpt. New York: Crowell, 1976.

A sound critical study with emphasis on an examination of the predominant themes in LOTR.

332. Foster, Robert. *A Guide to Middle Earth*. Baltimore: Mirage, 1971. 291pp.

This essential reference book is a concordance to LOTR, containing a glossary of all the proper names that appear therein, as well as in *The Hobbit, The Adventures of Tom Bombadil,* and *The Road Goes Ever On.*

333. Grotta-Kurska, Daniel. *J.R.R. Tolkien: Architect of Middle Earth*. Philadelphia: Running Press, 1976. 165pp.

Grotta-Kurska, a professional journalist, has produced a readable and fairly accurate biography of Tolkien. The writing style is journalistic and suffers at times from a lack of revision as well as errors in fact (which could have been corrected if source material had been re-checked), indicating both author and publisher were hurried by a tight deadline--that of preceding the Carpenter biography. The book's poor layout, typos, chopped references, and indications of deleted material tend to support this assumption. As he was denied access to Tolkien's papers, family members, and friends ("I learned that the family had requested Tolkien's close friends and associates to refrain from giving me information out of respect to Tolkien's memory"), his work relies on the public record and the aid of those who knew Tolkien and agreed with Grotta-Kurska's position. Considering the conditions existing at the time of writing, Grotta-Kurska has produced an admirable study. His biography seems scrupulously fair in its tone, and he carefully states his approach, methodology, and sources (indeed, the book is more adequately referenced than Carpenter's). The book is of value for its account of Tolkien's literary reputation, the controversy surrounding the publication of LOTR in America, and the growth of the Tolkien cult, as well as providing some balanced (though debatable) assessments of Tolkien's writings and their literary significance.

334. Helms, Randel. *Tolkien's World*. Boston: Houghton Mifflin, 1974. 167pp.

A controversial literary study which applies Freudian analysis to the characters and themes of Middle-earth. Helms explores the nature of Tolkien's "creative imagination" with a study of the evolution of his conception of Middle-earth, "an independent realm of the imagination with its own laws and significances, and with, as well, a strange relevance to our own world."

335. Kilby, Clyde S. *Tolkien & The Silmarillion*. Wheaton, IL: Harold Shaw, 1976. 89pp.

Kilby, a former chairman of the English Department of Wheaton College and an authority on the work and thought of C.S. Lewis and Tolkien, here describes a summer spent with the latter to read and to aid him in preparing *The Silmarillon* for publication. He provides a fascinating glimpse of the elderly Tolkien. To these personal observations, Kilby has added a valuable chapter on the personal and literary relationship of Tolkien to C.S. Lewis and Charles Williams.

336. Kocher, Paul. *Master of Middle-earth: The Achievement of J.R.R. Tolkien.* Boston: Houghton Mifflin, 1972. 247pp.

An excellent study of Tolkien's major fiction. Discusses the ideas of morality and social order underlying Tolkien's works, with emphasis on LOTR, but considering his other writings as well. Especially illuminating are two chapters which discuss the cosmic order and the races that make up the Fellowship of the Ring. A balanced analysis which remains the best book-length study of Tolkien's writings.

337. Lobdell, Jared, ed. *A Tolkien Compass.* La Salle, IL: Open Court, 1975. 201pp.

Ten essays on Tolkien's writings, with emphasis on LOTR and *The Hobbit.* One of the most valuable contributions to this volume is Tolkien's own "Guide to the Names in *The Lord of the Rings,*" a series of notes (slightly edited for publication by Christopher Tolkien) which he prepared for translators.

338. Noel, Ruth S. *The Mythology of Middle-earth.* Boston: Houghton Mifflin, 1977. 198pp.

Noel, a student of mythology, is convincing and fascinating as she connects Tolkien's fantasies with the myths of the ancient world. The book is divided into four parts: themes, places, beings, and things. In the creation of his mythology Tolkien drew upon his vast knowledge of early mythology, but his final creation was based on a combination of mythic tradition and the imagination of a 20th century Englishman. Includes a glossary, a brief bibliography, and an index.

339. Tyler, J.E.A. *The Tolkien Companion.* London: Macmillan, 1976. 531pp. Rpt. New York: St. Martin's Press, 1976.

A compilation of almost every known fact, name, "foreign" word, date, and etymological allusion occuring in Tolkien's history of Middle-earth. Includes a detailed guide to the various Elvish writing systems, together with explanatory maps,

charts, and genealogical tables developed by the
compiler and drawn by Kevin Reilly. A valuable concordance which provides a fascinating entry into
Tolkien's world.

340. West, Richard C. *Tolkien Criticism: An Annotated
Checklist*. [Kent, OH]: Kent State University
Press, 1970. 73pp.

A checklist of the writings by and about Tolkien.
Divided into three sections: Section A, containing
Tolkien's writings, including books and contributions to books and periodicals (this list is not
complete); Section B, an annotated listing of critical writings on Tolkien in books, periodicals,
and newspapers (purposely omits, with one exception,
all material appearing in amateur journals, including *The Tolkien Journal* and *Mythlore*); Section C,
listing reviews of Tolkien's works (not annotated);
Index by title of material in Section B. An updated
and expanded edition is needed with at least selected
amateur magazine contributions and book reviews annotated. A more comprehensive checklist of Tolkien's
writings is Humphrey Carpenter, *Tolkien: A Biography*
(which see).

ALFRED ELTON VAN VOGT

341. Van Vogt, A.E. *Reflections of A.E. Van Vogt: The
Autobiography of a Science Fiction Giant, With
a Complete Bibliography*. Lakemont, GA: Fictioneer
Books, 1975. 136pp.

This autobiography is based upon a transcript of a
twelve-hour interview recorded in 1961 by Elizabeth
Dixon of UCLA for an oral history program sponsored
by Columbia University and the Berkeley and Los
Angeles campuses of the University of California.
Van Vogt states that he revised and updated the
transcript, but "tried to retain the original oral
flavor." An awkward, rambling, and confused book.
It is a revealing look at the author of *Slan* and as
such it is regretable that he allowed its publication. A checklist of van Vogt's books and periodical
contributions is included.

JULES VERNE

342. Allott, Kenneth. *Jules Verne*. London: Cresset Press,
     1940. 283pp. Rpt. Port Washington, NY: Kennikat
     Press, 1970.

     The first English-language biography. Leans heavily
     on a study by Verne's niece, Marguerite Allottee de
     la Fuye's *Jules Verne--sa Vie, son Oeuvre* (Kra,
     1928). A competent chronological biography and as-
     sessment which is still of value.

343. Chesneaux, Jean. *The Political and Social Ideas of
     Jules Verne*. London: Thames and Hudson, 1972.
     224pp.

     A detailed analysis of Verne's "Voyages Extraordin-
     aires" which relates them to the political and social
     theories of 19th century France. Includes a selected
     bibliography and an index.

344. Jules-Verne, Jean. *Jules Verne: A Biography*. New
     York: Taplinger, 1976. 245pp.

     This biography by Verne's grandson was originally
     published in French in 1973. For this edition the
     translator, Roger Greaves, adapted the text (with
     the author's permission), including rearrangements,
     deletions, and additions. Verne destroyed his per-
     sonal files in 1898 and Jean Jules-Verne has made
     inspiring use of surviving manuscripts, letters,
     and other material from family archives. There are
     numerous valuable summaries of Verne's lesser known
     works which, along with the detailed life and Verne's
     own statements on the evolution of many of his tales,
     will aid modern scholars in their assessment of
     Verne's role in the development of modern science
     fiction. Jean Jules-Verne also places Verne's works
     into the social and political context of his era.
     One of Greaves' most useful additions was to supply
     a comprehensive checklist of Verne's major published
     (and surviving unpublished) writings in books and
     periodicals, citing the first printing as well as
     all known English translations, and an extensive
     list of writings in books and periodicals about
     Verne and his work. This work should be considered
     the standard biography.

KURT VONNEGUT, JR.

345. Giannone, Richard. *Vonnegut: A Preface to his Novels.*
    Port Washington, NY: Kennikat Press, 1977. 136pp.

    A chronological study of Vonnegut's eight novels,
    from *Player Piano* to *Slapstick*, designed to provide
    "a systematic inquiry into the features of Vonnegut's
    novelistic art as it develops."

346. Goldsmith, David H. *Kurt Vonnegut: Fantasist of Fire
    and Ice.* Bowling Green, OH: Bowling Green Univer-
    sity Popular Press, 1972. 44pp. [paper].

    An examination of Vonnegut's themes and literary
    techniques with an assessment of the reasons for
    his acceptance as a writer of importance.

347. Klinkowitz, Jerome and John Somer, eds. *The Vonnegut
    Statement.* New York: Delacorte Press, 1973. 286pp.

    Thirteen pieces which provide an assessment of Vonne-
    gut the public figure and literary phenomenon and of
    Vonnegut's writings and literary significance twenty
    years after the publication of his first book. Div-
    ided into three parts--the public figure, the liter-
    ary figure, and the literary art--the essays offer a
    broad study of Vonnegut and his work. Topics covered
    include his popular acceptance as a paperback writer,
    as a nationally prominent figure, and as a hero of
    college youth; his literary expertise dating from
    his own college days through his academic acceptance
    and popular acclaim; and the treatment of six novels
    and many stories. Includes the text of an October
    1966 interview of Vonnegut by Robert Scholes. De-
    tailed bibliography, but superseded by Pieratt and
    Klinkowitz (which see).

348. Pieratt, Asa B., Jr. and Jerome Klinkowitz. *Kurt
    Vonnegut, Jr.: A Descriptive Bibliography and
    Annotated Secondary Checklist.* [Hamden, CT]:
    Archon Books, 1974. 138pp.

    The most complete bibliography of writings by and
    about Vonnegut to date. The main section is a des-
    criptive bibliography listing Vonnegut's books in
    chronological order with title page transcriptions,
    physical details, contents listing, and full details
    on all known printings and foreign editions in Eng-
    lish and other languages. Other sections list short
    fiction, poetry, drama, essays, reviews, introduc-
    tions, forewords, and published speeches in other

publications, as well as interviews, discussions, recorded remarks, student contributions to the *Cornell Sun*, dramatic and cinematic adaptations of his work, and letters and manuscripts. The annotated checklist of secondary material lists work on Vonnegut's writings in books, portions of books, periodicals (including little magazines), and newspapers. Additionally, non-annotated sections cover biographical notations of, and reviews of books by Vonnegut, doctoral dissertations, and bibliographies. Indexed.

349. Reed, Peter J. *Kurt Vonnegut, Jr.* New York: Warner Paperback Library, 1972. 222pp. [paper]. Rpt. New York: Thomas Y. Crowell, 1976.

A literary study of the six novels, *Player Piano, The Sirens of Titan, Mother Night, Cat's Cradle, God Bless You, Mr. Rosewater,* and *Slaughterhouse-Five, or The Children's Crusade,* written by Vonnegut between 1952 and 1969.

STANLEY G. WEINBAUM

350. De la Ree, Gerry and Sam Moskowitz, eds. *After Ten Years: A Tribute to Stanley G. Weinbaum, 1902-1935.* Westwood, NJ: Gerry de la Ree, 1945. [paper].

Contains an autobiographical sketch; selections from Weinbaum's letters; memoirs by Margaret Weinbaum Kay and Helen Weinbaum; notes on the unpublished novel, *The Mad Brain*; an essay by Moskowitz; and a checklist of Weinbaum's fiction.

HERBERT GEORGE WELLS

351. Bergonzi, Bernard. *The Early H.G. Wells: A Study of the Scientific Romances.* Toronto: University of Toronto Press, 1961. 226pp.

The seminal study of Wells as a literary artist. Bergonzi considers Wells' fiction through 1901 (with the exception of a few later stories), the year he published *The First Men in the Moon,* his last genuine novel-length romance, and *Anticipations,* his first major work of non-fiction, where he ceased to be an artist and began his long career as publicist and pamphleteer. Bergonzi outlines the *fin de*

siecle intellectual attitude which dominated Wells'
novels and stories of the 1890s and places his early
work in the literary context of the period. He terms
Wells' fictional work of the 1890s romances in the
tradition of Hawthorne, rather than scientific fiction in the tradition of Verne. He refers to Wells'
early romances as myths reflecting some of the dominant preoccupations of the *fin de siecle* period.
Bergonzi fully justifies his claim for Wells as an
artist and thus lays the groundwork for the reinter-
pretation of his science fiction as well as his other
fiction. Appended to the study are two of Wells'
early fictions, "A Tale of the Twentieth Century"
and "The Chronic Argonauts"; the latter, a fragment
of a fantastic novel written at the age of twenty-
one, is the earliest draft of *The Time Machine*.
Indexed.

352. Bergonzi, Bernard, ed. *H.G. Wells: A Collection of
     Critical Essays*. Englewood Cliffs, NJ: Prentice-
     Hall, 1976. 182pp.

Ten essays which provide a survey of the key criti-
cal insights that produced the present revaluation
of Wells' fiction. Five of these deal with the sci-
ence fiction: "Disentanglement as a Theme in H.G.
Wells's Fiction" by Robert P. Weeks, "The Scientific
Romances" by V.S. Pritchett, "*The Time Machine*: An
Ironic Myth" by Bernard Bergonzi, "The Logic of
'Prophecy' in *The Time Machine*" by Robert M. Philmus,
and "Through the Novelist's Looking-Glass" by Gloria
Glikin Fromm.

353. Dickson, Lovat. *H.G. Wells: His Turbulent Life and
     Times*. London: Macmillan, 1969. 330pp.

This work has largely been superseded by the MacKenzie biography (which see) but remains valuable for
its account of the relationship between Wells and
the Macmillans.

354. Hammond, J.R. *Herbert George Wells: An Annotated
     Bibliography of His Works*. New York: Garland
     Publishing, 1977. 257pp.

A descriptive bibliography of the works of H.G. Wells
and the most comprehensive listing on Wells published
to date. Divided into the following categories: romances and novels, short stories, essays (published
in book form), non-fiction (books and pamphlets),
collected editions, posthumously published works,
and letters. Within each category, the listing is
chronological.

Annotations are included for all first editions,
and where original editions have subsequently been
revised, full details are given. Appendices on the
works of H.G. Wells, chronologically arranged; notes
on unreprinted writings; critical, biographical, and
bibliographical studies; principal collections of
H.G. Wells material; and the H.G. Wells Society.
Indexed.

355. Hillegas, Mark R. *The Future as Nightmare*. (See
III B2)

356. H.G. Wells Society, The. *H.G. Wells: A Comprehensive
Bibliography*. London: H.G. Wells Society, 1966.
61pp. 2nd ed. London: H.G. Wells Society, 1968.
70pp. 3rd ed., with new index. London: H.G. Wells
Society, 1972. 74pp.

A comprehensive checklist of the first printings of
Wells' books and pamphlets. Includes a useful synopsis for each entry. Appendices include: short
stories by Wells with original appearances noted;
a comprehensive, but incomplete, list of miscellaneous writings by and about Wells; film and stage
adaptations; and a biographical outline of Wells.

357. Mackenzie, Norman and Jeanne. *The Time Traveller:
The Life of H.G. Wells*. London: Weidenfeld and
Nicolson, 1973. 487pp. Rpt. *H.G. Wells: A Bio-
graphy*. New York: Simon and Schuster, 1973.

Not perfect, but an indispensable biography based
in part on "unrestricted access to the Wells Archive" at the University of Illinois at Champaign-
Urbana. Select chronological checklist of Wells'
books. Indexed.

358. Parrinder, Patrick. *H.G. Wells*. Edinburgh: Oliver
and Boyd, 1970. 120pp.

A critical study of Wells' major fiction through
1912. Not indexed.

359. Parrinder, Patrick, ed. *H.G. Wells: The Critical
Heritage*. London: Routledge & Kegan Paul, 1972.
351pp.

A selection of writings on Wells from 1895 to 1946
by Joseph Conrad, E.M. Forster, Henry James, Virginia
Woolf, T.E. Lawrence, F.R. Leavis, T.S. Eliot, and
others. Included is a reprint of Zamyatin's aston-
ishing short book, *Herbert Wells* (Petersburg, 1922),
which provides the key to why *We* appears so anti-
Wellsian.

360. Philmus, Robert M. *Into the Unknown*. (See III B3)

361. Suvin, Darko with Robert M. Philmus, eds. *H.G. Wells and Modern Science Fiction*. Lewisburg: Bucknell University Press, 1977. 279pp.

Nine essays, most of which were first presented during an international symposium on Wells held at McGill University in 1971, plus a general intro- duction by editor Suvin. The unifying theme of the essays is that modern science fiction originates from Wells. Contents: "The Folktale, Wells, and Modern Science Fiction" by Tatyana Chernysheva, "The Garden in Wells's Early Science Fiction" by David Y. Hughes, "Evolution As a Literary Theme in H.G. Wells's Science Fiction" by J.P. Vernier, "A Grammar of Form and a Criticism of Fact: *The Time Machine* as a Structural Model for Science Fiction" by Darko Suvin, "'I Told You So': Wells's Last Dec- ade, 1936-1945" by R.D. Mullen, "Imagining the Future: Wells and Zamyatin" by Patrick Parrinder, "The Shadow of *Men Like Gods*: Orwell's *Coming Up for Air* as Parody" by Howard Fink, "Borges and Wells and the Labyrinths of Time" by Robert M. Philmus, and "H.G. Wells and Japanese Science Fiction" by Sakyo Komatsu. In addition to the essays the book includes two important annotated checklists: the first, a selected bibliography of Wells' science journalism by David Y. Hughes and Robert M. Philmus, compliments the Mullen list and includes a number of articles not previously identified as by Wells; and the other, a survey of Wells' books and pamphlets in which com- piler R.D. Mullen presents an overview of Wells' fiction and non-fiction. Essential reading for stu- dents of Wells.

362. Wagar, W. Warren. *H.G. Wells and the World State*. New Haven, CT: Yale University Press, 1961. 301pp. Rpt. Freeport, NY: Books for Libraries Press, 1971.

A study of Wells' response to the economic, politi- cal, and spiritual crisis of the 20th century. In- dispensible to any full understanding of Wells.

363. Watkins, A.H., ed. *Catalogue of the H.G. Wells Collection in the Bromley Public Libraries*. Bromley: London Borough of Bromley Public Libraries, 1974. 196pp.

This checklist of 1290 entries comprising the H.G. Wells collection housed in the library of the Lon- don borough in which Wells was born in 1866 is an important asset to Wellsian studies. The checklist is divided into nine sections: the writings of Wells (including books, contributions to books, contributions to periodicals, and collected editions); bibliographies; catalogues; dictionaries; biography; books and articles relating to Wells other than biography; reviews of books by and about Wells; periodicals; letters (this section is annotated with summaries and/or quotations of the letters); pictorial material; and miscellany.

364. Wells, Geoffrey H. *The Works of H.G. Wells 1887-1925: A Bibliography, Dictionary, and Subject-Index*. London: Routledge, 1926. 274pp. Rpt. New York: Burt Franklin, 1970.

The most valuable feature of this work is the descriptive bibliography which lists Wells' books and pamphlets in chronological order with title page transcriptions, physical details, contents listing, notations of later editions, and miscellaneous notes. Other sections contain annotated checklists of unreprinted writings (regretably this section, though helpful, is simply a title listing without reference to the periodicals in which they were originally printed), letters published in newspapers, a note on foreign translations, an incomplete list of parodies of Wells, and critical studies of Wells in books, portions of books, and periodicals. The concordance to Wells' writings is valuable for its references to, and annotations of, practically every subject, fiction and non-fiction, upon which he has written.

365. Williamson, Jack. *H.G. Wells: Critic of Progress*. Baltimore: Mirage Press, 1973. 162pp.

This work is a revision of Williamson's doctoral dissertation, originally written in 1962-63. It is a solid contribution to Wells scholarship and remains one of the best places to begin the study of Wells' early fiction. Includes a bibliography and an index.

TERENCE HANBURY WHITE

366. Crane, John K. *T.H. White*. New York: Twayne Publishers, 1974. 202pp.

A biographical study of the author of *The Once and Future King*. Contains a primary bibliography.

367. Warner, Sylvia Townsend. *T.H. White: A Biography*.
     London: Jonathan Cape, 1967. 352pp.

     The indispensible life of White, which makes gener-
     ous use of his journals, diaries, and letters, as
     well as conversations with his friends. Emphasis is
     on details of biography, not a literary analysis of
     his writings.

CHARLES W.S. WILLIAMS

368. Glenn, Louis. *Charles W.S. Williams: A Checklist*.
     [Kent, OH]: Kent State University Press, 1975.
     128pp.

     To date the most comprehensive checklist of writings
     by and about Williams. The first section arranges
     Williams' writings chronologically in order of pub-
     lication in five categories: books; poems and stor-
     ies; articles and letters; reviews; and edited works.
     Provides publication information for each entry in-
     cluding first and successive appearances or editions
     and a note suggesting the nature of the work. The
     second section is an annotated list of works about
     Williams and his writings in books, portions of
     books, periodicals, and graduate research. A select-
     ed non-annotated listing of reviews of Williams'
     books is also present. A separate section listing
     dissertations and three indices are provided for
     cross-reference.

EVGENY ZAMYATIN

369. Brown, E.J. *Brave New World, 1984, and We: An Essay
     on Anti-Utopia*. Ann Arbor: Ardis Publishers,
     1977. 61pp.

     An essay on Zamyatin's art, philosophy and themes
     as well as an analysis of the ways in which modern
     literature--Western and Russian--has dealt with the
     problems of technology and social regimentation.
     Contains a selected bibliography of works by Zam-
     yatin in English translation and a checklist of
     works about Zamyatin.

V. PERIODICALS

A.   SCIENCE FICTION/FANTASY JOURNALS & MAGAZINES

370. *Algol: The Magazine about Science Fiction*. Ed.
     Andrew Porter. Box 4175, New York, NY 10017.

     One of the best of the semi-professional magazines
     of comment on science fiction. Includes feature
     articles by SF writers and critics, book reviews,
     interviews, and regular columns on SF art and fan-
     dom.

371. *Ariel*. Ed. Thomas Durwood. The Morning Star Press,
     Box 6011, Leawood, KS 66206.

     A profusly illustrated magazine with a strong em-
     phasis on heroic, sword and sorcery fantasy. Con-
     tains original fiction and art, and criticism of
     both literature and art.

372. *Cinefantastique*. Ed. Frederick S. Clarke. Box 270,
     Oak Park, IL 60603.

     A magazine devoted entirely to the science fiction,
     fantasy and horror film. Features major articles on
     recent films, as well as studies of film directors'
     works. Additional content includes film reviews and
     previews, and reviews of books on genre films. Su-
     perbly illustrated.

373. *CSL: The Bulletin of the New York C.S. Lewis
     Society*. Ed. Eugene McGovern. 9 Bradshaw
     Drive, Ossining, NY 10562.

     The monthly newsletter of the New York C.S. Lewis
     Society. Focuses primarily on Lewis' life, his
     writings, and his theology.

374. *Dark Horizons*. Ed. Geoffrey Noel Smith. The British
     Fantasy Society, c/o Brian Mooney, 447a Porters
     Av., Dagenham, Essex, RM9 4ND, England.

     The major publication of the British Fantasy Society.
     Includes original fiction and poetry, criticicm,
     and original art work.

375. *Delap's F&SF Review*. Ed. Richard Delap. 11863 West
Jefferson Blvd., Culver City, CA 90230.

A review journal devoted exclusively to science
fiction and fantasy. Includes fiction, non-fiction,
media arts, paperbacks, and juvenile titles.

376. *Extrapolation: A Journal of Science Fiction and
Fantasy*. Ed. Thomas D. Clareson. Box 3186,
The College of Wooster, Wooster, OH 44691.

The official journal of the MLA Seminar on Science
Fiction, also serving the Science Fiction Research
Association. The first academic journal for scholars
and teachers in the field.

377. *Foundation: the review of science fiction*. Ed. Peter
Nicholls. Longbridge Road, Essex RM8 2AS, England.

The journal of the [British] Science Fiction Foundation. Noteworthy for its scholarly reviews of new
books, and its series on the craft of science fiction by SF authors.

378. *Locus: The Newspaper of the Science Fiction Field*.
Ed. Charles N. and Dena Brown. Box 3938, San
Francisco, CA 94119.

An indispensable publication for those who desire
regular information on the current happenings in
the field on all levels.

379. *Luna*. Ed. Ann F. Dietz. 655 Orchard St., Oradell,
NJ 07649.

Regular features include: interviews with SF/F writers, reviews of adult and juvenile SF, a listing
of SF articles published in popular and library magazines, complete list of new books published in
hardcover and paperback in the U.S. and Britain.

380. *Mythlore: A Journal of J.R.R. Tolkien, C.S. Lewis,
and Charles Williams Studies*. Ed. Glen H. Good-
Knight. The Mythopoetic Society, Box 4671,
Whittier, CA 90607.

Contains historical and critical articles focusing
on the three writers and their circle, the Inklings.

381. *Orcrist: A Journal of Fantasy in the Arts* [and] *The Bulletin of the University of Wisconsin Tolkien Society*. Ed. Richard West. 1922 Madison St., Madison, WI 53711.

Focuses primarily on Tolkien with occasional pieces on other fantasy writers. Includes original fiction, poetry, music, and critical articles.

382. *Riverside Quarterly*. Ed. Leland Sapiro. Box 14451, University Station, Gainesville, FL 32604.

A "little magazine" of critical articles by academics, writers, and fans.

383. *The Science-Fiction Collector*. Ed. J. Grant Thiessen. 943 Maplecroft Road SE, Calgary, Alberta T2J 1W9 Canada.

A magazine for the collector and serious reader. Emphasis is on bibliography and reference. An important source for SF paperback checklists.

384. *Science-Fiction Studies*. Ed. R.D. Mullen and Darko Suvin. English Department, Indiana State University, Terre Haute, IN 47809.

One of two scholarly journals on science fiction published in the U.S. Articles are critical, theoretical, and bibliographic in nature.

385. *SF Commentary*. Ed. Bruce Gillespie. GPO Box 5195AA, Melbourne, Victoria 3001, Australia. American agents: Hank and Lesleigh Luttrell, 525 West Main, Madison, WI 53703.

An outstanding fanzine, distinguished by its quality reviews and by its special issues devoted to individual authors.

386. *SF Horizons*. Ed. Brian Aldiss and Harry Harrison. Rpt. New York: Arno Press, 1975.

The first scholarly journal of science fiction, established in 1964. Ceased publication after two issues for lack of financial and academic support.

387. *Xenophile*. Ed. Nils Hardin. Box 9660, St. Louis, MO 63122.

Carries articles on fantasy, science fiction, and supernatural horror pulp magazines.

B. SPECIAL ISSUES

388. *Fresco: The University of Detroit Quarterly.*
Detroit, MI: University of Detroit, Spring
1958.

The Howard Phillips Lovecraft Memorial Symposium,
comprising biographical and critical articles on
Lovecraft and his writings. Contributors include
Fritz Leiber, August Derleth, Joseph Payne Brennan,
David H. Keller, and others.

389. *Journal of the American Studies Association of
Texas.* Plainview, TX: Wayland College, 1973.

A special issue on the future of America, with
several essays on utopias and science fiction.

390. *Journal of General Education.* University Park, PA:
Pennsylvania State University, Spring 1976.

The whole devoted to nine papers on science fiction
delivered at the annual meeting of the Science
Fiction Research Association held at Penn State
in September 1973. The conference was a landmark
in the development of academic respectability for
SF criticism.

391. *Journal of Popular Culture.* Bowling Green, OH:
Popular Culture Association, Spring 1972.

Nine essays on science fiction, including an important discussion of *Astounding* magazine by Albert I.
Berger, "The Magic That Works: John W. Campbell and
the American Response to Technology."

392. *Mosaic: A Journal for the Comparative Study of
Literature & Ideas.* Winnepeg, Canada: University
of Manitoba, Winter 1977.

A special issue on "Faerie, Fantasy, and Pseudo-
Mediaevalia in Twentieth-Century Literature."
Essays on J.R.R. Tolkien, T.H. White, Ursula K.
Le Guin, and some fantasy subjects.

393. *The Shaw Review.* University Park, PA: Pennsylvania
State University, May 1973.

Special "G.B.S. and Science-Fiction" issue. Includes
essays by J.O. Bailey, Julius Kagarlitski, J.R.
Christopher, and others. Shaw/Science Fiction checklist compiled by John R. Pfeiffer.

394. *Studies in the Literary Imagination*. Atlanta, GA: Georgia State University, Fall 1973.

A special issue on "Aspects of Utopian Fiction." Contributors include Robert M. Philmus, David Ketterer, and Darko Suvin.

VI. SOURCES FOR ACQUISITION

A. DIRECTORIES

(1) General

395. *Bookdealers in North America: A Directory of Dealers in Secondhand and Antiquarian Books in Canada and the United States of America 1976-78.* 7th ed. London: Sheppard Press, 1976.

Contents: geographical list of dealers, alphabetical index, specialty section, and permanent want lists.

396. *A Directory of Dealers in Secondhand and Antiquarian Books in the British Isles 1973-75.* rev. ed. London: Sheppard Press, 1973.

Contents: geographical list of dealers, alphabetical index, specialty section, and permanent want lists.

(2) Science Fiction

397. Halpern, Frank M. *International Classified Directory of Dealers in Science Fiction and Fantasy Books and Related Materials.* Haddonfield, NJ: Haddonfield House, 1975. 90pp.

A useful directory of more than 130 specialists. Subject index to 297 areas of expertise.

B. BOOK DEALERS

398. Fantasy Centre, 43 Station Road, Harlesden, London NW10 4UP England.

399. L.W. Currey Rare Books Incorporated, Elizabethtown, NY 12932.

400. F. and S.F. Book Co., Box 415, Staten Island, NY
     10302.

401. Ferret Fantasy, Ltd., 27 Beechcroft Road, Upper
     Tooting, London SW17 England.

402. Kaleidoscope Books, 1792 Shattuck Ave., Berkeley,
     CA 94709.

403. Barry R. Levin, 2253 Westwood Blvd., Los Angeles,
     CA 90064.

404. Bertram Rota, 30 & 31 Long Acre, London WC2E 9LT
     England. (General new booksellers who stock
     British SF.)

DOCTORAL DISSERTATIONS IN SCIENCE FICTION AND FANTASY

by Douglas R. Justus

A large body of scholarship in the fields of science fiction and fantasy literature is to be found in Ph.D. dissertations. What follows is a bibliography of U. S. dissertations, as well as some British, Canadian, and Australian, that are concerned with science fiction, fantasy, and related subjects. The sources for this list are *A List of American Doctoral Dissertations; American Doctoral Dissertations; Index to American Doctoral Dissertations; Dissertations in English and American Literature; Guide to Dissertations in Victorian Literature 1886-1958;* and *Dissertation Abstracts International.* This bibliography represents an examination of these sources as of January 1977. For the convenience of the reader who desires a description of individual dissertations, references to *Dissertation Abstracts International* (DAI) and *Dissertation Abstracts* (DA) are provided.

A special debt of gratitude is owed H. W. Hall and his pioneering "Science Fiction Theses and Dissertations: a Preliminary Checklist," which appeared in the June-July 1975 issue of the *SFRA Newsletter*, with an addenda in the February-March 1976 issue.

Adam, Eugene Alfred. "A Structural Study of the Major
    Novels of John Cowper Powys." University of Cali-
    fornia, 1975; DAI, 36 (1975), 2211A.

Adams, Frank Davis. "The Literary Tradition of Scientific
    Romance." University of New Mexico, 1951.

Albrecht, Wilbur T. "William Morris' *The Well at the
    World's End:* An Explanation and a Study." University
    of Pennsylvania, 1970; DAI, 31 (1971), 5347A.

Allen, Elizabeth Estelle. "The Prose Romances of William
    Morris." Tulane University, 1975; DAI, 36 (1975),
    2211A.

Alterman, Peter Steven. "A Study of Four Science Fiction
    Themes and Their Function in Two Contemporary
    Novels." University of Denver, 1974; DAI, 35 (1974),
    2976A.

Ames, Russell. "Citizen Thomas More and His Utopia."
    Columbia University, 1949.

Anderson, Karl Oscar Emanuel. "Scandinavian Elements in
    the Works of William Morris." Harvard University,
    1942.

Anderson, Ray Lynn. "Persuasive Functions of Science-
    Fiction: A Study in the Rhetoric of Science." Uni-
    versity of Minnesota, 1968.

Aninger, Thomas. "The Essay Element in the Fiction of
    Aldous Huxley." University of California at Los
    Angeles, 1968; DAI, 29 (1968), 892A.

Antippas, Andy Peter. "The Burden of Poetic Tradition, a
    Study in the Works of Keats, Tennyson, Arnold and
    Morris." University of Wisconsin, 1968; DAI, 28
    (1968), 4591A.

Arnold, Joseph H., Jr. "Narrative Structure in *The Col-
    lected Tales of E. M. Forster.*" University of Illi-
    nois at Urbana-Champaign, 1973; DAI, 34 (1975),
    7908A.

Arons, Peter Lederman. "The Romanticism of James Branch
    Cabell." Yale University, 1964.

Arscott, Christine M. "A Study of *The Life and Death of
    Jason, The Earthly Paradise* and *Sigurd the Volsung,*
    with Special Reference to Morris's Treatment of His
    Sources." University of London—External, 1928.

117

Austin, Marvin Fraley. "The Novels of Kurt Vonnegut, Jr.: A Confrontation With the Modern World." University of Tennessee, 1975; DAI, 36 (1975), 3707A.

Baehr, Stephen Lessing. "The Utopian Mode in Eighteenth-Century Russian Panegyric Poetry." Columbia University, 1972.

Baily, James O. "Scientific Fiction in English, 1817-1914. A Study of Trends and Forms." University of North Carolina, 1934.

Barber, Dorothy Elizabeth Klein. "The Structure of *The Lord of the Rings*." University of Michigan, 1965; DA, 27 (1966), 470A.

Barnes, Myra Jean Edwards. "Linguistics and Languages in Science Fiction-Fantasy." East Texas State University, 1971; DAI, 32 (1972), 5210A.

Barshay, Robert Howard. "Philip Wylie: The Man and His Work." University of Maryland, 1975; DAI, 36 (1975), 3707A.

Bedient, Calvin B. "The Fate of the Self, Self and Society in the Novels of George Eliot, D. H. Lawrence and E. M. Forster." University of Washington at Seattle, 1964; DA, 25 (1964), 1187.

Bellamy, John Edward. "James Branch Cabell, A Critical Consideration of His Reputation." University of Illinois, 1954.

Bellas, Ralph A. "William Morris' Treatment of Sources in *The Earthly Paradise*." University of Kansas, 1960; DA, 22 (1961), 857.

Bentley, Joseph Goldridge. "Aldous Huxley and the Anatomical Vision." Ohio State University, 1961; DA, 22 (1962), 3655.

Berger, Harold Lynde. "Anti-Utopian Science Fiction of the Mid-Twentieth Century." University of Tennessee, 1970; DAI, 32 (1971), 420A.

Bierly, Charles E. "*Eureka* and the Drama of Self, A Study of the Relationship Between Poe's Cosmology and His Fiction." University of Washington at Seattle, 1957; DA, 18 (1958), 228.

Birnbaum, Milton. "Aldous Huxley, A Study of His Quest for Values." St. Louis University, 1956; DA, 17 (1957), 360.

Black, Judith Booher. "A Critical Look at William Morris' Guenevere." University of Miami, 1975; DAI, 36 (1975), 2836A.

Blake, George Baty, Jr. "Autobiography and Romance: The English Novels of John Cowper Powys." New York University, 1973; DAI, 34 (1973), 1271A.

Bleich, David. "Utopia, The Psychology of a Cultural Fantasy." New York University, 1968; DAI, 30 (1970), 4935A.

Blum, Irving, D. "Avarice in English Utopias and Satires from 1551 to 1714." Rutgers University, 1953.

Bodden, Rodney Vernon. "Modern Fantastic Fiction in Argentina." University of Wisconsin, 1970; DAI, 31 (1970), 1261A.

Bolling, Douglas Townshend. "Three Romances by Charles Williams." University of Iowa, 1970; DAI, 31 (1971), 4755A.

Borrello, Alfred. "H. G. Wells' Art of the Novel." St. John's University, 1965.

Boss, Edgar W. "The Theology of C. S. Lewis." Northern Baptist Theological Seminary, 1948.

Bowen, Roger. "Isolation, Utopia, and Anti-Utopia: The Island Motif in the Literary Imagination. A Selective History of the Archetype and Its Characteristics. With Special Studies in H. G. Wells, Joseph Conrad, and William Golding." Harvard University, 1972.

Bowersox, Hermann Clay. "Aldous Huxley, The Defeat of Youth." University of Chicago, 1943.

Bray, Mary Katherine. "The Outward Sense." University of Colorado, 1973; DAI, 34 (1973), 1893A.

Brebner, John Alexander. "The Demon Within: A Study of John Cowper Powys' Novels." University of New Brunswick, 1972; DAI, 33 (1972), 1715A.

Bromberger, Fredrick S. "William Morris's Concepts of Ideal Human Society as Indicated in Public Lectures, 1877-1894, and in Three Prose Romances, 1886-1890." University of Southern California, 1964; DA, 25 (1964), 3550.

Brostowin, Patrick Ronald. "John Adolphus Etzler: Scientific-Utopian During the 1830's and 1840's." New York University, 1969; DAI, 31 (1970), 864A.

Brown, Rexford Glenn. "Conflict and Confluence: The Art of Anthony Burgess." University of Iowa, 1971; DAI, 32 (1972), 5220A.

Browning, William Gordon. "Anti-Utopian Fiction: Definition and Standards for Evaluation." Louisiana State University, 1966; DA, 27 (1966), 1360.

Buchwald, Emilie. "The Earthly Paradise and the Ideal Landscape: Studies in a Changing Tradition, Through 1750." University of Minnesota, 1971; DAI, 32 (1971), 1465A.

Buckley, David Patrick. "The Novels of George Orwell." Columbia University, 1962; DA, 26 (1966), 7310.

Buckstead, Richard Chris. "Wells, Bennett, Galsworthy, Three Novelists in Revolt Against the Middle Class." University of Iowa, 1960.

Bursey, Wallace. "Rider Haggard: A Study in Popular Fiction." Memorial University of Newfoundland, 1973; DAI, 35 (1975), 4503A.

Burt, Donald Charles. "Utopia and the Agrarian Tradition in America, 1865-1900." University of New Mexico, 1973; DAI, 34 (1974), 7182A.

Calhoun, Catharine Blue. "The Pastoral Aesthetic of William Morris: A Reading of *The Earthly Paradise*." University of North Carolina at Chapel Hill, 1972; DAI, 33 (1972), 1137A.

Canary, Robert H. "The Cabellian Landscape: A Study of the Novels of James Branch Cabell." University of Chicago, 1964.

Canning, George Rolland, Jr. "William Morris, Man and Literary Artist." University of Wisconsin, 1958; DA, 19 (1959), 1753.

Caplan, Jay Louis, "The Voyage of the Imaginary." Yale University, 1973; DAI, 34 (1974), 7182A.

Carlock, Nancy E. "An Analysis of Utopian Concepts in Selected Nineteenth Century Fiction." Occidental College, 1964.

Carmassi, Guido Remo. "The Expanding Vision: Changes in Emphasis in William Morris' Late Prose Romances." University of Notre Dame, 1975; DAI, 36 (1976),5312A.

Carnell, Corbin Scott. "The Dialectic of Desire, C.S. Lewis' Interpretation of Sehnsucht." University of Florida, 1960; DA, 20 (1960), 4653.

Carr, Edward F. "Satiric Fantasy in English Fiction." University of Pittsburgh, 1953.

Carter, Albert Howard, III. "Fantasy in the Work of Italo Calvino." University of Iowa, 1972; DAI, 32 (1972), 5223A.

Chandler, John Herrick. "Charles Williams, The Poet of the Co-Inherence." University of Chicago, 1964.

Chen, Karl Chia. "A Study of the Sources and Influences Upon William Morris's The Defence of Guenevere and Other Poems." Yale University, 1934; DAI, 30 (1969), 1977A.

Choudhury, A.F. "The Enemy Territory, A Study of Joseph Conrad, E.M. Forster and D.H. Lawrence in Relation to Their Portrayal of Evil." Leicester [U.K.], 1968.

Christensen, Bonniejean McGuire. "Beowulf and The Hobbit: Elegy into Fantasy in J.R.R. Tolkien's Creative Technique." University of Southern California, 1969; DAI, 30 (1970), 4401A.

Christensen, John Michael. "Utopia and the Late Victorians: A Study of Popular Literature, 1870-1900." Northwestern University, 1974; DAI, 35 (1975), 6705A.

Christopher, Joe Randell. "The Romances of Clive Staples Lewis." University of Oklahoma, 1968; DAI,30 (1970), 3937A.

Clareson, Thomas Dean. "The Emergence of American Science Fiction: 1880-1915; A Study of the Impact of Science upon American Romanticism." University of Pennsylvania, 1956; DA, 16 (1956), 962.

Clough, Raymond Joseph. "The Metal Gods: A Study of the Historical and Mythic Aspects of the Machine Image in French Prose from 1750 to 1940." State University of New York at Buffalo, 1973; DAI, 34 (1974), 5959A.

Cockshott, Gerald W. "Music, and the Relationship Between Music and Nature in the Works of Aldous Huxley." London [U.K.], 1975.

Cohen, John Arthur. "An Examination of Four Key Motifs Found in High Fantasy for Children." Ohio State University, 1975; DAI, 36 (1976), 5016A.

Cohen, Morton Norton. "H. Ridder Haggard-His Life and Works." Columbia University, 1958; DA, 19 (1958), 324.

Cole, Susan Ablon. "The Utopian Plays of George Bernard Shaw: A Study of the Plays and Their Relationship to the Fictional Utopias of the Period from the Early 1870's to the Early 1920's." Brandeis University, 1972; DAI, 32 (1972), 6966A.

Collins, Denis Eugene. "Two Utopians: A Comparison and Contrast of the Educational Philosophies of Paulo Freire and Theodore Brameld." University of Southern California, 1973; DAI, 34 (1974), 4078.

Concannon, Gerald J. "The Development of George Orwell's Art." University of Denver, 1973; DAI, 34 (1973), 3386A.

Coogan, Robert Martin. "More's Utopia and the Christian Humanism in Petrarch's Latin Prose." Loyola University [Chicago], 1967.

Cook, David Allen. "The Quest for Identity in John Cowper Powys: A Reading of His Wessex Series." Pennsylvania State University, 1971; DAI, 34 (1972), 4606A.

Cornwell, Charles Landrum. "From Self to the Shire: Studies in Victorian Fantasy." University of Virginia, 1972; DAI, 33 (1972), 1163A.

Coughlan, Jeremy Sister. "The Pre-Raphaelite Aesthetic and the Poetry of Christina Rossetti, William Morris, and William Butler Yeats." University of Minnesota, 1967; DA, 28 (1967), 622A.

Crews, Fredrich C. "E.M. Forster, An Historical and Critical Study." Princeton University, 1958; DA, 19 (1959), 2951.

Crouch, Laura Ernestine. "The Scientist in English Literature: Domingo Gonsales (1638) to Victor Frankenstein (1817)." University of Oklahama, 1975; DAI,
36 (1975), 2181A.

Crowley, Cornelius Patrick. "A Study of the Meaning and
Symbolism of the Arthurian Poetry of Charles
Williams." University of Michigan, 1952; DA, 12
(1952), 185.

Cullen, John C. III. "The Literary Criticism of Charles
Williams." University of Texas at Austin, 1974;
DAI, 35 (1974), 2985A.

Cullinan, John Thomas. "Anthony Burgess' Novels: A Critical Introduction." Columbia University, 1972;
DAI, 35 (1975), 7900A.

Cunningham, Richard Bryan. "The Christian Apologetic of
C.S. Lewis." Southern Baptist Theological Seminary
[Louisville, Kentucky], 1966; DA, 27 (1966), 242A.

Curzon, Gordon A. "Paradise Sought: A Study of the Religious Motivation in Representative British and
American Literary Utopias, 1850-1950." University
of California at Riverside, 1969; DAI, 30 (1970),
4405A.

Dailey, Jennie Ora Marriott. "Modern Science Fiction."
University of Utah, 1974; DAI, 35 (1974), 1095A.

Dawson, Lawrence Russell, Jr. "Charles Williams as Re-
viewer and Reviewed." University of Michigan, 1960;
DA, 20 (1960), 4659.

DeAraujo, Victor. "The Short Story of Fantasy: Henry
James, H.G. Wells, and E.M. Forster." University
of Washington, 1966; DA, 27 (1966), 200A.

DeLaRoche, Wayne William. "Privacy and Community in the
Writings of Lewis Carroll." Columbia University,
1975; DAI, 36 (1975), 3683A.

Demaria, Robert. "From Bulwer-Lytton to George Orwell,
the Utopian Novel in England 1870-1950." Columbia
University, 1959; DA, 20 (1959), 667.

Denington, Frances Barbara. "The Complete Book: An Inves-
tigation of the Development of William Morris's
Aesthetic Theory and Literary Practice." McMaster
University [Canada], 1976; DAI, 37 (1976), 2194.

Devin, Juliette C. "Meredith and the Scientific Conversa-
   tionalists, A Study in Intellectual Companionship."
   University of Iowa, 1945.

Digg, Sandra Elizabeth. "The Identification and Analysis
   of Contemporary and Universal Themes in Selected
   Books of Children's Literary Fantasy Published between 1965 and 1970." University of Chicago, 1971.

Dimeo, Richard Steven. "The Mind and Fantasies of Ray
   Bradbury." University of Utah, 1970; DAI, 31 (1971),
   3541A.

Dockery, Carl Dee. "The Myth of the Shadow in the Fantasies of Williams, Lewis, and Tolkien." Auburn University, 1975; DAI, 36 (1975), 3727A.

Dodge, Robert Kendall. "The Influence of Machines and
   Technology on American Literature of the Late Nineteenth and Early Twentieth Centuries." University
   of Texas, 1967; DA, 28 (1969), 4122A.

Dooley, David Joseph. "The Impact of Satire on Fiction,
   Studies in Norman Douglas, Sinclair Lewis, Aldous
   Huxley, Evelyn Waugh, and George Orwell." University
   of Iowa, 1955; DA, 15 (1955), 2203.

Dowie, William John, Jr. "Religious Fiction in a Profane
   Time: Charles Williams, C. S. Lewis and J. R. R.
   Tolkien." Brandeis University, 1970; DA, 31 (1970),
   2911A.

Dowrey, Amy Louise. "The Life and Works of J. H. Rosny
   Aine, 1856-1940." University of Michigan, 1950; DA,
   10 (1950), 122.

Duffey, Paula. "Form and Meaning in the Novels of George
   Orwell." University of Pennsylvania, 1967; DA, 28
   (1967), 1816A.

Duke, Jean Maurice. "James Branch Cabell's Library: A
   Catalogue." University of Iowa, 1968; DA, 28 (1968),
   3971A.

Dunlap, Benjamin Bernard, Jr. "The Search for Paradise:
   A Thematic Study of the Poems of William Morris."
   Harvard University, 1967.

Dykstra, Emmanuel David. "Aldous Huxley, The Development
   of a Mystic." University of Iowa, 1957; DA, 17
   (1957), 3013.

Edelheit, Steven J. "Dark Prophecies: Essays on Orwell
    and Technology." Brandeis University, 1975; DAI, 36
    (1975), 308.

Edrich, Emmanuel. "Literary Technique and Social Temper
    in the Fiction of George Orwell." University of Wis-
    consin, 1960; DA, 21 (1960), 620.

Ekstrom, William F. "The Social Idealism of William
    Morris and William Dean Howells: A Study of Four
    Utopian Novels." University of Illinois, 1947.

Eldridge, Shaila Van Sickle. "The 'Life by Value' in the
    Novels of E. M. Forster." University of Denver,
    1975; DAI, 36 (1975), 2842A.

Enroth, Clyde Adolph. "The Movement Toward Mysticism in
    the Novels of Aldous Huxley." University of Minne-
    sota, 1956; DA, 16 (1956), 1905.

Eurich, Nell P. "Science in Utopia, a Mighty Design: A
    Study of Scientific Utopias in the Seventeenth Cen-
    tury." Columbia University, 1959; DA, 20 (1960),
    4098.

Ewbank, David Robert. "The Role of Woman in Victorian
    Society: A Controversy Explored in Six Utopias,
    1871-1895." University of Illinois, 1968; DAI, 30
    (1969), 318A.

Fabbricante, Lorrie Victor. "J. H. Rosny Aine and His
    Novels: Social, Analytical and Prehistorical."
    Columbia University, 1953; DA, 14 (1954), 124.

Felsen, Hans Eugene. "The Function of Heresy in Modern
    Literature: Studies in the Major Fiction of Thomas
    Hardy, E. M. Forster, and D. H. Lawrence." Univer-
    sity of Maryland, 1974; DAI, 36 (1975), 1524A.

Fenerle, Lois Marie. "Goethe's *Wilhelm Meisters Wander-
    jahre:* A Document in the History of Utopian Thought."
    University of Kansas, DAI, 30 (1970), 5443A.

Fiderer, Gerald Lionel. "A Psychoanalytic Study of the
    Novels of George Orwell." University of Oklahoma,
    1967; DA, 28 (1967), 1074A.

Fink, H. R. "George Orwell's Novels in Relation to His
    Social and Literary Theory." London—University
    [U. K.], 1968.

Firchow, Peter Edgerly. "Aldous Huxley and the Art of Satire: A Study of His Prose Fiction to *Brave New World*." University of Wisconsin, 1965; DA, 26 (1966), 5433.

Fischer, Adam Jacob. "Formula for Utopia: The American Proletarian Novel, 1930-1939." University of Massachusetts, 1974; DAI, 35 (1974), 447A.

Fisher, Vivian Boyd. "The Search for Reality Through Dreams: A Study of the Work of William Morris from 1856 to 1872." Emory University, 1973; DAI, 34 (1973), 767A.

Foster, Mark Anthony. "Write the Other Way: The Correlation of Style and Theme in Selected Prose Fiction of Ray Bradbury." Florida State University, 1973; DAI, 34 (1973), 1906A.

Fraser, Joseph Hugh, Jr. "An Introduction to the Hermetic Novels of Charles Williams." Texas A & M University, 1975; DAI, 36 (1975), 2808A.

Friend, Beverly Oberfield. "The Science Fiction Fan Cult." Northwestern University, 1975; DAI, 36 (1976), 4475A.

Fry, Kenneth Richard. "The Victorian Decorative Impulse in the Poetry of William Morris." University of Missouri, 1966; DA, 27 (1967), 3452A.

Fry, Phillip L. "An Annotated Calendar of the Letters from E. M. Forster to Joe R. Ackerley in the Humanities Research Center, the University of Texas at Austin." Texas University at Austin, 1974; DAI, 35 (1974), 449A.

Fullman, Christopher Edward. "The Mind and Art of Charles Williams, A Study of His Poetry, Plays and Novels." University of Wisconsin, 1954.

Futch, Ken. "The Syntax of C. S. Lewis' Style: A Statistical Look at Some Syntactic Features." University of Southern California, 1969; DAI, 30 (1969), 2002A.

Gardner, Delbert Ralph. "William Morris's Poetic Reputation in England, 1858-1900." University of Rochester, 1963; DA, 24 (1963), 2030.

Garr, Alice Carol. "German Science Fiction: Variations on the Theme of Survival in the Space Time Continuum." University of North Carolina at Chapel Hill, 1973; DAI, 34 (1973), 2623A.

Gbenschikov, George Vladimir. "Ivan Efremov's Theory of Soviet Science Fiction." Michigan State University, 1972; DAI, 33 (1973), 7530A.

Gent, Margaret G. "Theme and Symbol in the Poetry of William Morris." Leeds [U. K.], 1970.

Gibson, Lary Hazelton. "The Disenchanted Garden, A Study of the Major Fiction of James Branch Cabell's The Biography of the Life of Manuel." University of Oregon, 1965; DA, 26 (1966), 5433.

Gigrich, John P. "An Immortality for Its Own Sake: A Study of the Concept of Poetry in the Writings of Charles Williams." Catholic University, Washington, 1954.

Gish, Robert Franklin. "Literary Allusion and the Homiletic Style of E. M. Forster: A Study in the Relationship Between the Tales and the Novels." University of New Mexico, 1972; DAI, 33 (1973), 5678A.

Glad, John Peter. "Russian Soviet Science Fiction and Related Critical Activity." New York University, 1970; DAI, 31 (1971), 6055A.

Gleaves, Robert Milnor. "Fantasy in the Contemporary Mexican Short Story: A Critical Study." Vanderbilt University, 1968; DA, 29 (1969), 2261A.

Going, Margaret Elizabeth Moorer. "John Cowper Powys, Novelist." University of Michigan, 1955; DA, 15 (1955), 582.

Goldsmith, David Hirsh. "The Novels of Kurt Vonnegut, Jr." Bowling Green State University, 1970; DAI, 31 (1970), 2916A.

Gooch, Velma L. "William Morris: Towards Unity in Art and Life." Manchester [U. K.], 1973.

Goodwin, K. L. "The Relationship Between the Narrative Poetry of William Morris, His Art and Craft-Work, and His Aesthetic Theories." Oxford University [U. K.], 1970.

Gordon, Walter K. "A Critical Selected Edition of William Morris's Oxford and Cambridge Magazine, 1856." Pennsylvania University, 1960; DA, 21 (1961), 3781.

Goshorn, James William. "The Queasy World of Kurt Vonnegut, Jr.: Satire in the Novels." University of New Mexico, 1971; DAI, 32 (1972), 6426A.

Gray, Charles Farrell, "The Theory of Literature of James Branch Cabell." University of Florida, 1966; DA, 27 (1967), 3455A.

Green, William Howard. "*The Hobbit* and Other Fiction by J. R. R. Tolkien: Their Roots in Medieval Heroic Literature and Language." Louisiana State University, 1969; DAI, 30 (1970), 4944A.

Greene, James J. "Thomas More and the More Tradition." Columbia University, 1966; DA, 27 (1967), 3840A.

Greenfield, Robert M. "Discursive Orwell." Columbia University, 1967; DA, 28 (1967), 1818A.

Greenlaw, Marilyn Jean. "A Study of the Impact of Technology on Human Values as Reflected in Modern Science Fiction for Children." Michigan State University, 1970; DA, 31 (1971), 5665A.

Greenwald, A. Michael. "William Cowper Powys's Fiction of Escape." Harvard University, 1974.

Grenewitz, Rainer Vadim. "Aspects of Romanticism in the 1920's in The Soviet Union: Zamyatim, Pilnyak, and Leonov." Cornell University, 1971; DAI, 32 (1972), 6976A.

Gross, Janet Sussman. "Ralph Robynson's Translation of Sir Thomas More's *Utopia*: A Critical Edition." University of North Carolina at Chapel Hill, 1971; DAI, 32 (1972), 5227A.

Gurko, Leo M. "Benda, Lewis, and the War Against Intellect." University of Wisconsin, 1935.

Hagarty, Ambrose W. "The Conical Bite—Swift's Influence on Orwell." Trinity—Dublin [U. K.], 1971.

Haigh, John D. "The Fiction of C. S. Lewis." Leeds [U. K.], 1963.

Hall, Larry Joe. "The Development of Myth in Post-World-War-II American Novels." North Texas State University, 1974; DAI, 35 (1975), 6139A.

Hall, Serena G. "George Meredith's Prose Fiction in the Light of His Theory of Comedy." Boston University, 1942.

Hamburger, Robert A., Jr. "Fiery Zeal: A Study of George Meredith's Fiction from *The Shaving of Shagpat* to *The Egoist*." University of Chicago, 1971.

Hamilton, Seymore C. "Towards a Human View of the Future: A Study of American Science Fiction Short Stories in Popular Magazines 1926-1960." Queens College [Canada], 1971.

Hammond, Evelyn B. "Aldous Huxley: Syncretic Synthesist." University of Southern California, 1974; DAI, 35 (1974), 3741A.

Hanawalt, Mary A.W. "The Attitude of Charles Kingsley Towards Science." University of Iowa, 1936.

Hansot, Elisabeth. "A Study in Classical and Modern Utopias." Columbia University, 1967; DAI, 31 (1970), 1856A.

Harms, Jean McLain. "Children's Responses to Fantasy in Relation to Their Stage of Intellectual Development." Ohio State University, 1972; DAI, 33 (1973), 6234A.

Harpham, Goeffrey Galt. "Cultural Degeneration and the Grotesque in H.G. Wells and Jack London." University of California at Los Angeles, 1974; DAI, 35 (1975), 5345A.

Harris, William Stryon, Jr. "Allegorical Techniques in Charles Kingsley's Novels." Duke University, 1971; DAI, 32 (1972), 3251A.

Hart, Dabney A. "C.S. Lewis, An Apology for Poetry." University of Wisconsin, 1959.

Hart, John Edward. "George Meredith, The Quest of Self, A Study of Mythical Pattern and Symbol." Syracuse University, 1954; DA, 14 (1954), 2345.

Hart, Lida D. "C.S. Lewis's Defense of Poesie." University of Wisconsin, 1958.

Hart, Thomas N. "G.K. Chesterton's Case for Christianity: A Critical Study." Graduate Theological Union, 1974; DAI, 35 (1974), 2384A.

Hawkins, Mark Frank. "The Late Prose Romances of William Morris, A Biographical Interpretation." University of California at Berkeley, 1969; DAI, 30 (1970), 4451A.

Hearron, William T. "New Approaches in Post-Modern American Novel: Heller, Vonnegut, and Brautigan." Buffalo University, 1973; DAI, 34 (1973), 3398A.

Heckathorn, John Gene. "The Early Novels of Aldous Huxley." University of Pennsylvania, 1975; DAI, 36 (1976), 5316A.

Hein, Rolland Neal. "Faith and Fiction: A Study of the Effects of Religious Convictions in the Adult Fantasies and Novels of George MacDonald." Purdue University, 1970; DAI, 32 (1971), 919A.

Henderson, Stephen Evangelist. "A Study of Visualized Detail in the Poetry of Tennyson, Rossetti, and Morris." University of Wisconsin, 1959; DA, 20 (1959), 1015.

Hergenhan, L. T. "A Critical Consideration of the Reviewing of the Novels of George Meredith, from *The Shaving of Shagpat* to *The Egoist*." London—Birkbeck [U. K.], 1960.

Herzog, Ronald Martin. "From Castle to Commune: A Study of Expanding Consciousness in the Novels of Aldous Huxley." City University of New York, 1974; DAI, 35 (1974), 1657A.

Hewitt, Christian Blanchard. "The Novels of John Cowper Powys." Boston University, 1961; DA, 22 (1961), 870.

Hillegas, Mark Robert. "The Cosmic Voyage and the Doctrine of Inhabited Worlds in Nineteenth Century English Literature." Columbia University, 1957; DA, 17 (1957), 2001.

Higgins, James Edward. "Five Authors of Mystical Fancy for Children: A Critical Study." Columbia University, 1965; DA, 26 (1966), 4629.

Hines, Joyce Rose. "Getting Home: A Study of Fantasy and the Spiritual Journey in the Christian Supernatural Novels of Charles Williams and George MacDonald." City University of New York, 1972; DAI, 33 (1972), 755A.

Hirsch, Walter. "American Science Fiction, 1926-1950. A Content Analysis." Northwestern University, 1957; DA, 17 (1957), 3113.

Hoare, A. D. "The Works of Morris and of Yeats in Relation to Early Saga Literature." Cambridge [U. K.], 1930.

Hoey, Mary A. "An Applied Linguistical Analysis of the Prose Style of C. S. Lewis." University of Connecticut, 1966; DA, 27 (1967), 3441A.

Hoff, Jacobo E. "The Idea of God and Spirituality of C. S. Lewis." Pontifica Universitas Gregoriana Facultas Theologica, 1969.

Hollow, John W. "Singer of an Empty Day: William Morris and the Desire for Immortality." University of Rochester, 1969; DAI, 30 (1970), 3461A.

Holmes, Charles Mason, II. "The Novels of Aldous Huxley." Columbia University, 1959; DA, 20 (1960), 3743.

Howard, Thomas T. "Charles William's Experiment in the Novel." New York University, 1970; DA, 31 (1970), 1760A.

Howells, C. A. "The Presentation of Emotion in the English Gothic Novels of the Late Eighteenth and Early Nineteenth Centuries, With Particular Reference to Ann Radcliffe's *Mysteries of Udolpho*, M. G. Lewis' *Monk*, Mary Shelley's *Frankenstein*, C. R. Mathin's *Melmoth the Wanderer*, Charlotte Bronte's *Jane Eyre*, and Works by Minor Minerva Press Prose Novelists Regina Maria Roche and Mary Anne Radcliffe." London Royal Holloway [U. K.], 1969.

Hunter, Jefferson Estock. "George Orwell and the Uses of Literature." Yale University, 1973; DAI, 34 (1973), 2629A.

Hussey, John Patrick. "Ascent and Return: The Redemptive Voyage of Poe's Hero." University of Florida, 1971; DAI, 32 (1972), 6979A.

Ingraham, Vernon Leland. "The Verse Drama of Charles Williams." University of Pennsylvania, 1965; DA, 26 (1966), 7318.

Jackson, Alan Steward. "George Orwell's Utopian Vision." University of Southern California, 1965; DA, 26 (1965), 2215.

Jago, D. M. "Tradition and Progress in Shaw and Wells, Belloc and Chesterton." Liecester [U. K.], 1965.

James, William Closson. "Christian Epic Heroism: A Study of *Beowulf*, *Paradise Regained*, and *The Lord of the Rings*." University of Chicago, 1974.

Jayaraman, T. "The Relation Between Art and Ideas in the Development of Aldous Huxley." Leeds [U. K.], 1966.

Johnson, C. R. "A Critical Study of the Novels of Bulwer-Lytton." Oxford [U. K.], 1973.

Johnson, Roy R. "A Critical Study of H. G. Wells' Development and Reputed Decline as a Novelist." Exeter [U. K.], 1973.

Jyoti, D. D. "Mystical and Transcendental Elements in Some Modern English and American Writers in Relation to Indian Thought, R. W. Emerson, H. D. Thoreau, E. M. Forster, T. S. Eliot, A. Huxley." London—Kings [U. K.], 1957.

Kamsi, S. N. "English Sociological Fiction, 1827-55, The Contributions of Six Predeccessors and Contemporaries of Dickens—Harriet Martineau, Frances Trollope, Charlotte Elizabeth, Benjamin Disraeli, Elizabeth Gaskell, Chas. Kingsley." Manchester [U. K.], 1966.

Kearse, Lee Andrew, Jr. "George Orwell: Romantic Utopian." Brown University, 1973; DAI, 34 (1974), 6593A.

Kegel, Charles Herbert. "Medieval-Modern Contrasts Used for a Social Purpose in the Work of William Corbett, Robert Southey, A. Welby Pugin, Thomas Carlyle, John Ruskin, and William Morris." Michigan State University, 1955; DA, 15 (1955), 2526.

Kellman, Martin Hirsh. "Arthur and Others: The Literary Career of T. H. White." University of Pennsylvania, 1973; DAI, 34 (1973), 1917A.

Kerpneck H. "Image, Symbol and Myth in the Novels of George Meredith." University of Toronto, 1966; DA, 28 (1967), 1399A.

Khan, S. W. "Indian Elements in the Works of Yeats, Eliot and Huxley." Nottingham [U. K.], 1956.

Khanna, Lee Cullen. "More's *Utopia*: A Literary Perspective on Social Reform." Columbia University, 1969; DAI, 30 (1969), 1530A.

Kirlin, Thomas Michael. "H. G. Wells and the Geometric Imagination: A Study of Three Science Fiction Novels in the Nineties." University of Iowa, 1974; DAI, 35 (1974), 2276A.

Klein, Mary Anne. "Conceptual and Artistic Limits of Eight Nineteenth Century British Literary Utopias." Marquette University, 1973; DAI, 35 (1974), 1048A.

Knapp, John Victor. "George Orwell: An Evaluation of His Early Fiction." University of Illinois, 1971; DAI, 32 (1972), 5794A.

Kubal, David Lawrence. "Outside the Whale: George Orwell's Search for Meaning and Form." University of Notre Dame, 1968; DA, 29 (1968), 265A.

Kumler, Alden D. "Aldous Huxley's Novel of Ideas." University of Michigan, 1957; DA, 18 (1958), 1432.

Kuyk, Dirk A., Jr. "Strategies of Unreason." Brandeis University, 1970; DAI, 32 (1971), 440A.

La Croix, J. F. "Lord Dunsany." Trinity—Dublin [U. K.], 1956.

Lagerwey, Wallace Peter. "Hans Henry Jahnn's *Ugrino und Ingrabanien*: Utopia and Its Failure." Northwestern University, 1974; DAI, 35 (1974), 3749A.

Lancaster, Robert Vaughan. "The Letters of John Cowper Powys to Louis Wilkinson, 1957-1963." Syracuse University, 1974; DAI, 36 (1975), 320A.

Larson, Ross Frank. "Fantasy and Imagination in the Mexican Narrative." University of Toronto, 1973; DAI, 35 (1974), 1108A.

Laverty, Carroll D. "Science and Pseudo-Science in the Writings of Edgar Allan Poe." Duke University, 1951.

Lea, Sydney L. W., Jr. "Gothic to Fantastic: Readings in Supernatural Fiction." Yale University, 1972; DAI, 34 (1973), 323A.

LeBourgeois, John Young. "The Youth of William Morris, 1834-76: An Interpretation." Tulane University, 1971; DAI, 32 (1971), 2035A.

Leclair, Thomas Edmund. "Final Words: Death and Comedy in the Fiction of Donleavy, Hawkes, Barth, Vonnegut, and Percy." Duke University, 1972.

Lee, Lawrence Lynn. "The Moral Themes of E. M. Forster." University of Utah, 1959; DA, 20 (1959), 1790.

Lee, Robert Alan. "The Spanish Experience, George Orwell and the Politics of Language." University of Oregon, 1967; DA, 27 (1967), 3053A.

LeGates, Charlotte Jane. "Aldous Huxley and Visual Art." Michigan State University, 1974; DAI, 35 (1975), 6144A.

Leitenberg, Barbara. "The New Utopias." Indiana University, 1975; DAI, 36 (1976), 5282A.

LeMire, Eugene Dennis. "The Unpublished Lectures of
    William Morris, A Critical Edition, Including an
    Introductory Survey and a Calendar and Bibliography
    of Morris's Public Speeches." Wayne State University,
    1962; DA, 24 (1964), 3325.

Letson, Russell Francis. "The Approaches to Mystery: The
    Fantasies of Arthur Machen and Algernon Blackwood."
    Southern Illinois University, 1975; DAI, 36 (1976),
    8047A.

Liberman, Michael Raymond. "William Morris's *News From
    Nowhere*: A Critical and Annotated Edition." Univer-
    sity of Nebraska, 1971; DAI, 32 (1972), 3956A.

Litte, Bruce Randolph. "John Cowper Powys: The Reputa-
    tion of the Novelist in England and America." Uni-
    versity of Kansas, 1974; DAI, 35 (1975), 6146A.

Litzengerg, Karl. "Contributions of the Old Norse Lan-
    guage and Literature to the Style and Substance of
    the Writings of William Morris, 1858-1876." Univer-
    sity of Michigan, 1933.

Lockridge, Ernest Hugh. "Aldous Huxley and the Novel of
    Diversity." Yale University, 1964; DA, 25 (1965),
    4703.

Lonie, Charles Anthony. "Accumulations of Silence: Sur-
    vivor Psychology in Vonnegut, Twain and Hemingway."
    University of Minnesota, 1974; DAI, 35 (1975), 7871A.

Lott, Hershel Woodley. "The Social and Political Ideals
    in the Major Writings of T. H. White." University of
    Southern Mississippi, 1970; DAI, 31 (1971), 4126A.

Lourie, Margaret. "William Morris' *The Defence of
    Guenevere and Other Poems*: An Introduction With Cri-
    tical and Historical Commentary." University of
    Chicago, 1972.

Lyngstad, Sverre. "Time in the Modern British Novel,
    Conrad, Woolf, Joyce, and Huxley." New York Univer-
    sity, 1960; DA, 27 (1966), 1374.

Lyon, Laurence Gill. "German Literary Utopias of the
    Eighteenth-Century With Emphasis on the Period 1700-
    1740." Harvard University, 1974.

MacMinn, Ney L. "The Letters of William Morris to the
    Press, 1868-1895." Northwestern University, 1928.

Madlener, Alan Fred. "Primitivism and Related Ideas in the Literary Works of William Morris." University of California at Berkeley, 1973.

Mall, James Parker. "La Nouvelle Heloise: Rousseau's Fiction and the Impossibility of Utopia." University of Illinois, 1969; DAI, 30 (1969), 1569A.

Mann, Nancy Elizabeth Dawson. "George MacDonald and the Tradition of Victorian Fantasy." Stanford University, 1973; DAI, 34 (1973), 3414A.

Marshall, Donald Ray. "The Green Promise: Greenness as a Dominate Symbol for the Quest for Eden in American Fiction." University of Connecticut, 1971; DAI, 32 (1971), 925A.

Mathews, Richard B. "The Fantasy of Secular Redemption." University of Virginia, 1973; DAI, 34 (1974), 4211A.

Matter, William Ward. "Aldous Huxley and the Utopian Tradition." Texas Technical University, 1971; DAI, 33 (1972), 279A.

Maurer, Oscar E., Jr. "*The Earthly Paradise*, by William Morris." Yale University, 1935.

May, K.M. "The Novels of Aldous Huxley: A Study of the Bearing of Form and Style Upon Meaning." London [U.K.], 1971.

Mazer, Charles Litten. "Orwell's Oceania, Zamyatin's United State, and Levin's Unicomp Earth: Socially Constructed Anti-Utopias." Texas Technical University, 1975; DAI, 37 (1976), 957A.

McClintock, Michael William. "Utopias and Dystopias." Cornell University, 1970; DAI, 31 (1970), 394A.

McGillis, Rodrick. "The Fantastic Imagination: The Prose Romances of George MacDonald." Reading [U.K.], 1973.

McGinnis, Wayne Douglas. "Kurt Vonnegut, Jr.'s Confrontation With Meaninglessness." University of Arkansas, 1974; DAI, 35 (1974), 3753A.

McGregor, D.R. "Myth and Fantasy in Some Late Victorian Novelists With Special Reference to R.L. Stevenson and George MacDonald." Auckland [Australia], 1973.

McInnis, John Lawson, III. "H. P. Lovecraft: The Maze
and The Minotaur (Volumes 1 and 2)." Louisiana State
University, 1975; DAI, 36 (1975), 2207A.

McKensie, Patricia Alice. "*The Last Battle*: Violence and
Theology in the Novels of C. S. Lewis." University
of Florida, 1974; DAI, 36 (1975), 907A.

McMurry, Myra Kibler. "Self and World: The Problem of
Proportion in the Novels of George Meredith." Emory
University, 1972; DAI, 33 (1972), 2943A.

Meckier, Jerome Thomas. "Aldous Huxley: Satire and Structure." Harvard University, 1968.

Meerse, Peggy Currey. "The Idea of Order and the Process
of Experience in More's *Utopia*." University of Illinois, 1972; DAI, 34 (1973), 735A.

Meister, John G. H. "The Descent of the Irrelative One:
The Metaphysics and Cosmology of Edgar Allan Poe's
Eureka." University of Pennsylvania, 1969; DAI, 30
(1969), 2490A.

Mellichamp, Leslie R., Jr. "A Study of George Orwell:
The Man, His Import and His Outlook." Emory University, 1968; DAI, 30 (1969), 729A.

Mench, Martha Duvall. "The Argonautic Tradition in
William Morris' *The Life and Death of Jason*: A
Study in Poetic Eclecticism." Yale University, 1968;
DA, 29 (1968), 1212A.

Meyers, Carolyn H. "Psychotechnology in Fiction About
Imaginary Societies, 1923-1962." University of Ken-
tucky, 1965; DAI, 30 (1969), 2490A.

Miles, Gwyneth Frances. "The Interaction Between Landscape and Myth in the Novels of John Cowper Powys."
University of British Columbia [Canada], 1973; DAI,
34 (1974), 7768A.

Millman, Lawrence. "Rider Haggard and the Male Novel.
What is *Pericles?* Beckett Gags." Rutgers University,
1974; DAI, 35 (1975), 6675A.

Missey, James Lawrence. "Appearance and Reality in the
Fiction of E. M. Forster." University of Pennsylvania, 1963; DA, 24 (1963), 2037.

Mobley, Jane. "Magic is Alive: A Study of Contemporary
Fantasy Fiction." University of Kansas, 1974; DAI,
36 (1975), 881A.

Mobley, Jonnie Patricia. "Toward Logres: The Operation of Efficious Grace in Novels by C. S. Lewis, Charles Williams, Muriel Spark, and Gabriel Fielding." University of Southern California, 1973; DAI, 34 (1973), 4274A.

Moorman, Charles W. "Myth and Modern Literature, a Study of the Arthurian Myth in Charles Williams, C. S. Lewis, and T. S. Eliot." Tulane University, 1953.

Moran, Kataryn Lou. "Utopias, Subtopias, Dystopias in the Novels of Anthony Burgess." University of Notre Dame, 1974; DAI, 35 (1974), 2286A.

Morgan, Dean Lucien. "Scientific Method and Vision of Reality: The Short Stories of H. G. Wells." University of Southern California, 1967; DA, 28 (1968), 4182A.

Morris, J. A. "George Orwell's Portrayal of Collective Irrationalism." Nottingham [U. K.], 1971.

Mountjoy, Harry W. "The Comic Fantasy in English Fiction of the Victorian Period." University of Pennsylvania, 1934.

Muhawi, Ibrahim M. "A Study of Self and Other in the Novels of Aldous Huxley." University of California at Davis, 1969; DAI, 31 (1970), 2394A.

Mundhenk, Rosemary Karmlich. "Another World: The Mode of Fantasy in the Fiction of Selected Nineteenth Century Writers." University of California at Los Angeles, 1972; DAI, 33 (1973), 5688A.

Murphy, Michael William. "The British Tale in the Early Twentieth Century: Walter De La Mare, A. E. Coppard and T. F. Powys." University of Wisconsin, 1971; DAI, 32 (1971), 2098A.

Murray, Donald Charles. "A Study of the Novels of Aldous Huxley." Syracuse University, 1966; DA, 27 (1967), 4261A.

Neuleib, Janice Witherspoon. "The Concept of Evil in the Fiction of C. S. Lewis." University of Illinois, 1974; DAI, 35 (1975), 4539A.

Neumann, Bonnie Rayford. "Mary Shelley." University of New Mexico, 1972; DAI, 33 (1973), 5689A.

Newell, Kenneth B. "Structure in H. G. Wells' Dickensian Novels." University of Pennsylvania, 1965; DA, 28 (1967), 239A.

Newenschwander, Dennis Bramwell. "Themes in Russian Utopian Fiction: A Study of The Utopian Works of M. M.
Sheherbatov, A. Ulybyshev, F. V. Bulgarin and V. F.
Odoevstij." Syracuse University, 1974; DAI, 36
(1975), 282A.

Nierenberg, Edwin H. "Two Essayists on Man, Alexander
Pope and E. M. Forster." University of Pittsburgh,
1962; DA, 23 (1963), 4678.

Noonan, Gerald Andrew. "Idea and Technique in the Novels
of Aldous Huxley." University of Toronto, 1971; DAI,
32 (1971), 3320A.

Norwood, William Durward, Jr. "The Neo-Medieval Novels of
C. S. Lewis." University of Texas, 1965; DA, 21
(1961), 2221.

Novick, Sherwood Mitchell. "George Meredith: from *The
Shaving of Shagpat* to *The Egoist*." Washington University, 1973; DAI, 34 (1973), 1865A.

Nydahl, Joe Mellin. "Utopia Americana: Early American
Utopian Fiction, 1790-1864." University of Michigan,
1974; DAI, 35 (1975), 7263A.

Oberg, Charlotte, H. "The Pagan Prophet: Unity of Vision
in the Narrative Poetry of William Morris." University of Virginia, 1970; DAI, 31 (1971), 4786A.

O'Hare, Colman. "Charles Williams, C. S. Lewis and J. R.
R. Tolkien: Three Approaches to Religion in Modern
Fiction." University ofToronto, 1973; DAI, 36 (1975),
1532A.

Orth, Michael Paul. "Tarzan's Revenge: A Literary Biography of Edgar Rice Burroughs." Claremont Graduate
School, 1974; DAI, 35 (1974), 3002A.

Ozolins, Aija. "The Novels of Mary Shelley: from *Frankenstein* to *Falkner*." University of Maryland, 1972;
DAI, 33 (1972), 2389A.

Panage, John H. "Representative Late Nineteenth Century
English Utopias." University of Minnesota, 1939.

Pandey, Nand K. "The Influence of Hindu and Buddist
Thought on Aldous Huxley." Stanford University,
1964; DA, 25 (1964), 1921.

Parrinder, John P. "H. G. Wells and the Social Novel."
Cambridge [U. K.], 1970.

Pavich, Paul Nicholas. "Kurt Vonnegut, Jr.: Apostle to the Disillusioned." University of New Mexico, 1973.

Pechefsky, Howard Sheldon. "The Fantasy Novels of John Cowper Powys." New York University, 1971; DAI, 32 (1972), 4014A.

Peckham, Robert Wilson. "The Novels of Charles Williams." University of Notre Dame, 1965; DA, 26 (1966), 6049.

Penman, M. E. "Moments of Apperception in the Modern Novel, A Study of Henry James, Virginia Woolf, E. M. Forster and James Joyce Related to Psychiatric and Philosophic Developments in the Late Nineteenth and Early Twentieth Centuries." London—University [U. K.], 1966.

Petty, Anne Cotton. "The Creative Mythology of J. R. R. Tolkien: A Study of the Mythic Impulse." Florida State University, 1972; DAI, 33 (1972), 2390A.

Philmus, Robert Michael. "Into the Unknown, the Evolution of Science Fiction in England from Francis Godwin to H. G. Wells." University of California at San Diego, 1968; DA, 29 (1968), 1545A.

Poburko, Nicholas Stephen. "The Fiction of E. M. Forster." Harvard University, 1973.

Popescu, Constantin C. "Fantastic Elements in Nineteenth-Century American Prose." University of Wisconsin, 1973; DAI, 34 (1974), 7718A.

Poster, Mark Steven. "The Utopian Thought of Restif De La Bretonne." New York University, 1968; DAI, 30 (1969), 255A.

Potts, Willard Charles. "H. G. Wells on the Novel." University of Washington, 1969; DAI, 30 (1969), 2544A.

Powell, Judith Ann Ahrens. "Three Vanishing Values—Huxley's Permutations of 'The Tempest.'" University of Utah, 1973; DAI, 34 (1973), 1930A.

Powers, Katharine Richardson. "The Influence of William Godwin on the Novels of Mary Shelley." University of Tennessee, 1972; DAI, 33 (1973), 4359A.

Pratter, Fredrick Earl. "The Uses of Utopia: An Analysis of American Speculative Fiction, 1880-1960." University of Iowa, 1973; DAI, 35 (1974), 468A.

Quattrocki, Edward A. "Theme and Structure in Plato's *Republic* and More's *Utopia*." Loyola University at Chicago, 1967.

Quinonez, Sister Lora A. "The Concept of Man in Representative Dystopian Novels." University of Michigan, 1969; DAI, 30 (1969), 2038A.

Quissell, Barbara Carolyn. "The Sentimental and Utopian Novels of Nineteenth-Century America: Romance and Social Issues." University of Utah, 1973; DAI, 34 (1973), 1867A.

Raknem, I. "H. G. Wells' Fiction from 1887 to 1920 in the Light of the Literary Criticism of His Age." London—Birkbeck [U. K.], 1955.

Rankin, C. B. "The Critical Reception of the Art and Thought of George Orwell." London—Birkbeck [U. K.], 1965.

Ransom, Ellene. "Utopus Discovers America; or Critical Realism in American Utopian Fiction, 1798-1900. Vanderbilt University, 1946.

Reddy, Albert Francis, S. J. "The Else Unspeakable: An Introduction to the Fiction of C. S. Lewis." University of Massachusetts, 1972; DAI, 33 (1972), 2949A.

Reilly, Robert J. "Romantic Religion in the Work of Owen Barfield, C. S. Lewis, Charles Williams and J. R. R. Tolkien." Michigan State University, 1960; DA, 21 (1961). 3461.

Reis, Richard H. "George MacDonald's Fiction, A Study of the Nature of Realism and Symbolism." Brown University, 1962; DA, 28 (1967), 1446A.

Robinson, Erwin A. "The Influence of Science Upon George Meredith." Ohio State University, 1936.

Roemer, Kenneth M. "America as Utopia, 1888-1900: New Visions, Old Dreams." University of Pennsylvania, 1971; DAI, 32 (1972), 4538A.

Rogers, Deborah Champion Webster. "The Fictitious Characters of C. S. Lewis and J. R. R. Tolkien in Relation to Their Medieval Sources." University of Wisconsin, 1972; DAI, 34 (1973), 334A.

Rooney, Charles J., Jr. "Utopian Literature as a Reflection of Social Forces in America, 1865-1917." George Washington University, 1968.

Rosecrance, Barbara Benjamin. "Voice and Vision: The Passage of E. M. Forster." Brandeis University, 1976; DAI, 37 (1976), 994A.

Ross, Eugene G. "The American Novel of Fantasy." University of Virginia, 1949.

Rossi, Lee Donald. "The Politics of Fantasy: C.S. Lewis and J.R.R. Tolkien." Cornell University, 1972; DAI, 33 (1973), 5195A.

Rothfork, John. "New Wave Science Fiction Considered as a Popular Religious Phenomenon: A Definition and an Example." University of New Mexico, 1973; DAI, 35 (1974), 1670A.

Roulet, William Matthew. "The Figure of the Poet in the Arthurian Poems of Charles Williams." St. John's University, 1965; DA, 28 (1968), 2694A.

Ruppe, John P. "In Search of Common Humanity: A Critical Study of the Early Novels and Essays of George Orwell." Rutgers University, 1972; DAI, 32 (1972), 5244A.

Russell, Margaret. "The Utopian Theme in the English Romance of the 17th Century." Yale University, 1923.

Russell, Mariann Barbara. "The Idea of the City of God." Columbia University, 1965; DA, 26 (1965), 3350.

Ryan, J.S. "Modern English Myth-Makers, An Examination of the Imaginative Writings of Charles Williams, C.S. Lewis, and J.R.R. Tolkien." Cambridge University [U.K.], 1967.

Sadler, Frank Orin. "Science and Fiction in the Science Fiction Novel." University of Florida, 1974; DAI, 36 (1975), 883A.

Sadler, Glenn E. "The Poetry of George MacDonald." Aberdeen [U.K.], 1967.

Sadler, Jeffrey Allen. "The Politics of the Margin: Aldous Huxley's Quest for Peace." University of Wisconsin, 1973; DAI, 35 (1974), 415A.

Saine, Ute Muller. "Bernardin De Saint-Pierre's *Paul et Virginie*: From Social Utopia to Escape Novel." Yale University, 1971; DAI, 32 (1972), 7003A.

St. Clair, Gloria Anne Strange Slaughter. "Studies in the Sources of J. R. R. Tolkien's *The Lord of the Rings*." University of Oklahama, 1970; <u>DAI</u>, 30 (1970), 5001A.

Samaan, Angele Botrose. "The Novels of Utopianism and Prophecy, From Lytton, 1871, to Orwell, 1949, With Special Reference to Its Reception." London-Birkbeck [U.K.], 1963.

Samuelson, David Norman. "Studies in the Contemporary American and British Science Fiction Novel." University of Southern California, 1969; <u>DAI</u>, 30 (1969), 1181A.

Sanders, Joseph Lee. "Fantasy in the Twentieth Century British Novel." Indiana University, 1972; <u>DAI</u>, 33 (1973), 7640A.

Schatt, Stanley. "The World Picture of Kurt Vonnegut, Jr." University of Southern California, 1970; <u>DAI</u>, 31 (1970), 767A.

Schatzberg, Walter. "Scientific Themes in the Popular Literature and Poetry of the German Enlightenment, 1720-1760." Johns Hopkins University, 1966; <u>DAI</u>, 27 (1966), 1837A.

Schmerl, Rudolph Benjamin. "Reason's Dream: Anti-Totalitarian Themes and Techniques of Fantasy." University of Michigan, 1960; <u>DA</u>, 21 (1961), 2298.

Schneiderman, Beth Kline. "From Fantasy to Prophecy: A Study of the Fiction of E.M. Forster." Purdue University, 1973; <u>DAI</u>, 35 (1974), 475A.

Schulz, Joan Evelyn. "A Study of H.G. Wells' *In the Days of the Comet*." University of Illinois, 1963; <u>DA</u>, 24 (1964), 4200.

Schwalbe, Doris Jeanne. "H.G. Wells and the Superfluous Woman." University of Colorado, 1962; <u>DA</u>, 23 (1962), 2120.

Scura, Dorothy. "Ellen Glasgow and James Branch Cabell: The Record of a Literary Friendship." University of North Carolina, 1973.

Segal, Phillip D. "Imaginative Literature and the Atomic Bomb: An Analysis of Representative Novels, Plays, and Films from 1945 to 1972." Yeshiva University, 1973; <u>DAI</u>, 34 (1974), 5993A.

Shah, Syed A. "The Empire in the Writings of Kipling, Forster and Orwell." Edinburgh [U.K.], 1967.

Shahane, V. A. "A Study of the Works of E. M. Forster With Special Reference to His Place in the Tradition of the English Novel." Leeds [U.K.], 1958.

Shapiro, Barbara Linda. "Autobiography and the Fiction of H.G. Wells." Harvard University, 1973; DAI, 35 (1975), 5363A.

Shaw, William Gary. "Comic Absurdity and the Novels of Kurt Vonnegut, Jr." Oklahama State University, 1975; DAI, 36 (1976), 7427A.

Shively, James Ross. "Fantasy in the Fiction of H.G. Wells." University of Nebraska, 1955; DA, 15 (1955), 1402.

Shor, Ira Neil. "Vonnegut's Art of Inquiry." University of Wisconsin, 1971; DAI, 32 (1971), 3331A.

Short, Clarice Evelyn. "The Poetic Relationship of Keats and William Morris." Cornell University, 1941.

Shurter, Robert L. "The Utopian Novel in America, 1865-1900." Case Western Reserve University, 1936.

Siciliano, Sam Joseph. "The Fictional Universe in Four Science Fiction Novels: Anthony Burgess's *A Clockwork Orange*, Ursula Le Guin's *The Word for World Is Forest*, Walter Miller's *A Canticle for Leibowitz*, and Roger Zelazny's *Creatures of Light and Darkness*." University of Iowa, 1975; DAI, 36 (1976), 8053A.

Silver, Carole Greta. "No Idle Singer: A Study of the Poems and Romances of William Morris." Columbia University, 1967; DA, 28 (1967), 644A.

Slaughter, Gloria A. "Studies in the Sources of J.R.R. Tolkien's *The Lord of the Rings*." University of Oklahoma, 1970.

Smith, Jane S. "Identity as Change: The Protean Character in Nineteen- and Twentieth-Century Fiction." Yale University, 1974; DAI, 35 (1974), 2955A.

Smith, Lewis C. "The Decline of Utopian Literature in the Seventeenth Century." University of Iowa, 1950.

Smith, Morine B. "The Complex Vision: Analysis and Resolution of Duality in the Novels of John Cowper
Powys." Queens [Canada], 1971.

Smyer, Richard Ingram. "Structure and Meaning in the
Works of George Orwell." Stanford University, 1968;
DA, 29 (1968), 615A.

Snyder, Phillip John. "Doing the Necessary Task: The
Bourgeois Humanism of George Orwell." Western
Reserve University, 1964; DA, 25 (1965), 6636.

Sokkari, S. El Y. "The Prose Romances of William Morris."
Manchester [U.K.], 1953.

Solberg, Vistor. "Source Book of English and American
Utopias." Ohio State University, 1932.

Soldati, Joseph Arthur. "Configurations of Faust: Three
Studies in the Gothic (1798-1820): *Weiland, Frank-
enstein, Melmoth the Wanderer*." Washington State
University, 1972; DAI, 32 (1972), 6945A.

Somer, John Laddie. "Quick-Statis: The Rite of Initiation
in the Novels of Kurt Vonnegut, Jr." Northern Illinois University, 1971; DAI, 32 (1972), 4025A.

Spatt, Hartley Steven. "William Morris: The Languages
of History and Myth." Johns Hopkins University,
1975; DAI, 36 (1976), 4518A.

Speare, Morris Edmund. "The Political Novels, Its Development in the Nineteenth Century England from Robert
Plume Ward to Mr. H. G. Wells." Johns Hopkins University, 1923.

Spencer, William. "The Cosmic Riddle: A Study of Aldous
Huxley's Thought." Sussex [U.K.], 1971.

Squires, Edgar L. "The Necessity for Self-Awakening in
the Scientific Romances and Early Social Novels of
H. G. Wells." University of California at Davis,
1966; DA, 28 (1967), 243A.

Stallman, Robert Lester. "The Quest of William Morris."
University of Oregon, 1966; DA, 27 (1967), 3064A.

Stevens, Arthur Wilber. "George Orwell and Contemporary British Fiction of Burma, The Problem of Place." University of Washington at Seattle, 1957; DA, 18 (1958), 1799.

Stienberg, M. W. "Formative Influences on the Thought of H. G. Wells." University of Toronto, 1951.

Stinson, John J. "The Uses of the Grotesque and Other Modes of Distortion: Philosophy and Implication in the Novels of Iris Murdoch, William Golding, Anthony Burgess, and J. P. Donleavy." New York University, 1971; DAI, 32 (1971), 1533A.

Stokes, Elmore E., Jr. "William Morris and Bernard Shaw, A Socialist Artistic Relationship." University of Texas, 1951.

Stone, Donald O. "The Questing Spirit of James Branch Cabell: The Evolution of a Theme." Florida State University, 1969; DAI, 32 (1971), 3273A.

Stoneburner, Charles Joseph. "The Regimen of the Ship-Star. A Handbook for the Anathemata of David Jones." University of Michigan, 1966; DA, 27 (1967), 3472A.

Strauss, Sylvia. "H. G. Wells and America." Rutgers University, 1968; DA, 29 (1969), 2199A.

Stubbs, David Carson. "Love in the Writings of C. S. Lewis." Florida State University, 1968.

Stupple, Alexander James. "Utopian Humanism in American Fiction, 1888-1900." Northwestern University, 1971; DAI, 32 (1971), 3273A.

Sullivan, Harry Richards. "The Elemental World of John Cowper Powys." University of Georgia, 1960; DA, 21 (1961), 2300.

Surtz, Edward L. "Philosophy and Education in More's *Utopia*." Harvard University, 1948.

Sutherland, Robert Warren, Jr. "The Political Ideas of George Orwell: A Liberal's Odyssey in the Twentieth Century." Duke University, 1968; DA, 29 (1969), 4563A.

Swann, William Kirk, III. "The Techniques of Softening E. T. A. Hoffman's Presentation of the Fantastic." Yale University, 1971; DAI, 32 (1972), 7009A.

Sweetland, James Harvey. "American Utopian Fiction." University of Notre Dame, 1976; DAI, 37 (1976), 1727A.

145

Taha, T. M. "Aldous Huxley's Conversion from Frustration to Fulfillment Through Mysticism." Trinity-Dublin [U.K.], 1961.

Thal-Larsen, Margaret. "Political and Economic Ideas in American Utopian Fiction, 1868-1914." University of California at Berkeley, 1941.

Tharp, James Burton. "The Fantastic Short Story in France (1850-1900): The Evolution of a Modern Genre." University of Illinois, 1928.

Thomas, Dante. "A Bibliography of the Principal Writings of John Cowper Powys and Some Works About Him." State University of New York at Albany, 1971; DAI, 32 (1971), 2106A.

Thrash, Lois Glenn. "Thematic Use of the Characters in the Novels of Charles Williams." Texas Technical University, 1972; DAI, 33 (1973), 4436A.

Tinsley, Molly Best. "The Prose Style of E. M. Forster." University of Maryland, 1975; DAI, 36 (1976), 6717A.

Tornquist, Marie Therese. "Art, Science, and Propaganda in the Works of H. G. Wells." Columbia University, 1972; DAI, 33 (1973), 7680A.

Trefman, Sunny. "William Morris, The Modernization of Myth." New York University, 1968.

Treguboff, Zoe L. "A Study of the Social Criticism in Popular Fiction, A Content Analysis of Science Fiction." University of California at Los Angeles, 1955.

Tropp, Martin. "Mary Shelley's Monster: A Study of *Frankenstein*." Boston University Graduate School, 1973; DAI, 34 (1973), 1871A.

Trowbridge, Clinton. "The Twentieth Century British Supernatural Novel." University of Florida, 1958; DA, 18 (1958), 1800.

Urgang, Gunnar. "Shadows of Heaven: The Use of Fantasy in the Fiction of C. S. Lewis, Charles Williams, and J. R. R. Tolkien." University of Chicago, 1970.

Valentine, Kristin B. "A Patterned Imagination: William Morris' Use of Pattern in Decorative Design and the Last Prose Romances, 1883-1896." University of Utah, 1974; DAI, 35 (1974), 1777A.

146

Van Dellen, Robert J. "Politics in Orwell's Fiction."
Indiana University, 1973; DAI, 33 (1973), 6378A.

Van Lachene, Stephen R. "Five Essays on the Gothic Novel
from Horace Walpole to Mary Shelley." University of
Notre Dame, 1973; DAI, 34 (1974), 4220A.

Vasbinder, Samuel Holmes. "Scientific Attitudes in Mary
Shelley's *Frankenstein*: Newtonian Monism as a Basis
for the Novel." Kent State University, 1976; DAI,
37 (1976), 2842A.

Vaughan, Gilbert. "Humor in the Early Fiction of H. G.
Wells." University of Arkansas, 1968; DA, 29 (1969),
278A.

Vinocur, Jacob. "Aldous Huxley, Themes and Variations."
University of Wisconsin, 1958; DA, 19 (1958), 1392.

Voohees, Richard Joseph. "The Paradox of George Orwell."
Indiana University, 1958; DA, 19 (1958), 533.

Wagner, Kenyon Lewis. "Anthony Burgess's Mythopoetic
Imagination: A Study of Selected Novels (1956-1968)."
Texas Technical University, 1974; DAI, 35 (1975),
7926A.

Wahl, J. R. "Two Pre-Raphaelite Poets, Studies in the
Poetry and Poetic Theory of William Morris and D.G.
Rossetti." Oxford-Balliol [U.K.], 1954.

Walker, Steven Charles. "Narrative Technique in the Fiction of J.R.R. Tolkien." Harvard University, 1973.

Warncke, Wayne Warren. "George Orwell as a Literary
Critic." University of Michigan, 1965; DA, 27
(1966), 488A.

Watt, Donald James. "The Human Fugue: Thought and Technique in Four Novels of Aldous Huxley." University
of Connecticut, 1968; DA, 29 (1969), 2728A.

Weeks, Robert Percy. "H.G. Wells as a Sociological Novelist." University of Michigan, 1952; DA, 12 (1952),
314.

Weinstein, Sharon Rosenbaum. "Comedy and Nightmare: The
Fiction of John Hawkes, Kurt Vonnegut, Jr., Jerzy
Kosinski, and Ralph Ellison." University of Utah,
1971; DAI, 32 (1971), 3336A.

Wells, Arvin Robert. "Jesting Moses, A Study in Cabellian Comedy." University of Michigan, 1959; DA, 20 (1959). 1796.

Wetzel, Frank Jacob. "Psychology and the Utopian Individual in Three Novellas by Robert Musil: *Die Vollendung Einer Liebe, Tonka,* and *Die Amsel.*" Cornell University, 1972; DAI, 34 (1973), 1300A.

White, William Luther. "The Image of Man in C. S. Lewis." Northwestern University and Garrett Theological Seminary, 1968; DA, 29 (1969), 2354A.

Whitesel, George Edward. "Evolution as Metaphor: Patterns of Continuity in the Thought and Aesthetic of Aldous Huxley." Michigan State University, 1970; DAI, 31 (1971), 6027A.

Wickert, Max Albrecht. "Form and Archetype in William Morris, 1855-1870." Yale University, 1965; DA, 27 (1966), 489.

Wilde, Alan. "The World of E. M. Forster." Harvard University, 1958.

Williamson, John Stewart. "H. G. Wells, Critic of Progress, A Study of Early Science Fiction." University of Colorado, 1964; DA, 26 (1966), 5420.

Winning, Charles Del N. "The Ideal Society in Nineteenth-Century English Literature. A Study of Utopian Phantasies." New York University, 1932.

Wolfe, Gary Kent. "The Symbolic Fantasy in England." University of Chicago, 1972.

Wood, Doreen Anderson. "The Pattern in the Myth: Archetypal Elements in C. S. Lewis's *Till We Have Faces.*" University of Tulsa, 1976; DAI, 37 (1976), 1575.

Wooden, Warren Walter, Jr. "Sir Thomas More, Satirist: A Study of the *Utopia* as Menippean Satire." Vanderbilt University, 1971; DAI, 32 (1971), 938A.

Wright, Marjorie E. "The Cosmic Kingdom of Myth, A Study in the Myth-Philosophy of Charles Williams, C. S. Lewis and J. R. R. Tolkien." University of Illinois, 1960; DA, 21 (1961), 3464.

Wuletich, Sybil. "Poe, The Rationale of the Uncanny." Ohio State University, 1961; DA, 22 (1962), 3675.

Wyatt-Brown, Anne Marbury. "E. M. Forster and the Trans-
  formation of Comedy." Case Western Reserve University, 1972; DAI, 33 (1972), 1751A.

Young, Archibald Morrison. "Thomas More and the Humanist
  Dialogue." University of Toronto, 1973; DAI, 35
  (1974), 1131A.

Ziegler, Mervin L. "Imagination as Rhetorical Factor in
  Works of C. S. Lewis." University of Florida, 1974;
  DAI, 35 (1974), 1277A.

Zylstra, Sape Anne. "Charles Williams: An Analysis and
  Appraisal of His Major Work." Emory University,
  1969; DAI, 30 (1969), 4468A.

AUTHOR INDEX

This index includes all authors cited in the main entries. Authors listed in section IV A-B are not included in the index. Numbers refer to entry code number.

British Museum, 12.
Brosman, John, 188.
Brown, E.J., 369.
Bruccoli, Matthew J., 235.
Burger, Joanne, 25.
Burgess, M.R., 19.

Cameron, Alastair, 7.
Canney, James R., 312.
Carpenter, Humphrey, 330.
Carter, Lin, 131, 280.
Carter, Margaret L., 41, 98.
Cawelti, John G., 132.
Cazedessus, C.E., Jr., 72.
Chalker, Jack L., 33, 292, 322.
Chauvin, Cy, 133.
Chesneaux, Jean, 343.
Christopher, Joe R., 273.
Clarens, Carlos, 189.
Clareson, Thomas D., 95, 134, 135, 136, 196.
Clarke, Ignatius Frederick, 42, 43, 99.
Clipper, Lawrence J., 243.
Cockcroft, Thomas G.L., 58, 59, 323.
Cohen, Morton N., 255.
Cole, Walter R., 54.
Conover, Willis, 290.
Cook, W. Paul, 281.
Crane, John K., 366.
Crawford, Joseph H., 26.

Davenport, Basil, 137, 138.
Davis, Joe Lee, 236.
Day, Bradford M., 27, 28, 60, 61, 197, 304, 314.
Day, Donald B., 62.
De Bolt, Joe, 225.
De Camp, L. Sprague, 100, 101, 102, 139, 140, 263,
    264, 282.
De la Ree, Gerry, 350.
Del Rey, Lester, 152.
Delany, Samuel R., 141.
Derleth, August, 29, 247, 283, 284.
DeVore, Howard, 30.
Dickson, Lovat, 353.
Donahue, James J., 26.
Dozois, Gardner, 329.

Eichner, Henry M., 44, 103.
Eisgruber, Frank, Jr., 73, 183.
Ellik, Ronald, 326.
Elliott, Robert C., 104.
Ellis, S.M., 198.
Eschelbach, Claire John, 268.
Eshbach, Lloyd Arthur, 142.

Eurich, Nell, 105.
Evans, Robley, 331.
Evans, William, 67, 326.

Falconer, Lee N., 265.
Farson, Daniel, 327.
Foster, Robert, 332.
Franklyn, H. Bruce, 143.
Franson, Donald, 6, 30.
Frewin, Anthony, 152.
Frye, Borthrop, 144.

Gardner, Martin, 215.
Gattegno, Jean, 239.
Gerani, Gary, 190.
Gerber, Richard, 45, 106.
Gernsback, Hugo, 63.
Giannone, Richard, 345.
Gibb, Jocelyn, 274.
Gibson, R.W., 107, 303.
Gillespie, Bruce, 248.
Glenn, Louis, 368.
Glut, Donald F., 108, 109.
Goble, Neil, 209.
Goddard, James, 212.
Goldsmith, David H., 346.
Goldstone, Adrian, 299.
Goodman, Michael B., 233.
Goulart, Ron, 177.
Gove, Philip Babcock, 46, 110.
Grant, Donald M., 26, 285.
Green, Roger Lancelyn, 111, 275.
Greene, Douglas G., 216.
Grotta-Kurska, Daniel, 333.
Gunn, James, 145, 146.

H.G. Wells Society, The, 356.
Hadley, Thomas P., 285.
Hall, Graham, 218.
Hall, H.W., 186.
Hall, James N., 237.
Halpern, Frank M., 397.
Hammond, J.R., 354.
Hanff, Peter E., 216.
Harbottle, Philip, 254.
Harper, Andrew, 302.
Harrison, Harry, 195.
Harwood, John, 227.
Heartman, Charles F., 312.
Heins, Henry Hardy, 228.
Helms, Randel, 334.
Hillegas, Mark R., 112, 147, 199, 355.
Hoffman, Stuart, 74.

152

Hooper, Walter, 275.
Hudson, Derek, 240.

Indick, Benjamin P., 220.
Irwin, W.R., 148.

Johnson, William, 191.
Jones, Robert Kenneth, 64, 178, 179.
Jules Verne, Jean, 344.

Ketterer, David, 149.
Kilby, Clyde S., 335.
Klinkowitz, Jerome, 347, 348.
Knapp, Lawrence, 253.
Knight, Damon, 150, 151.
Kocher, Paul, 336.
Kuehn, Robert E., 269.
Kyle, David, 152.

Le Guin, Ursula K., 271.
Lee, Walt, 77.
Leighton, Peter, 113.
Lobdell, Jared, 337.
Locke, George, 31, 32, 47.
London, John, 279.
Long, Frank Belknap, 286.
Lord, Glenn, 266.
Lovecraft, Howard Phillips, 153, 287, 288, 289, 290.
Lowndes, Robert A.W., 154.
Ludlam, Harry, 328.
Lundwall, Sam J., 155.
Lupoff, Richard A., 229, 230.
Lyles, W.H., 316.

McAulay, George, 302.
MacDonald, Greville, 296.
McFall, Russell P., 213.
McGhan, Barry, 5.
Mackenzie, Jeanne, 357.
Mackenzie, Norman, 357.
McKinstry, Lohr, 71.
McNamee, Lawrence F., 86.
McNutt, Daniel J., 114.
Madan, Falconer, 241.
Manlove, C.N., 200.
Menville, Douglas, 192.
Metcalf, Norm, 65.
Metzger, Arthur, 310.
Miller, Marjorie M., 210.
Modern Humanities Research Association, 88.
Modern Language Association of America, 89.
Moore, Raylyn, 217.
Morse, A. Reynolds, 320.

Shober, Joyce Lee, 268.
Shreffler, Philip A., 294.
Sidney-Fryer, Donald, 324.
Siemon, Frederick, 56.
Silverberg, Robert, 51.
Slusser, George Edgar, 222, 251, 261, 272.
Small, Christopher, 306, 317.
Smith, Clark Ashton, 171.
Somer, John, 347.
Spelman, Richard C., 35, 36.
Starrett, Vincent, 300.
Steinhoff, William, 307.
Stone, Graham, 69.
Strauss, Erwin S., 70.
Strick, Philip, 194.
Sullivan, John, 244, 245.
Summers, Alphonse Montague, 52.
Suvin, Darko, 37, 160, 361.
Sweetser, Wesley, 299.
Swigart, Leslie Kay, 252.

Taylor, Angus, 249.
Todorov, Tzvetan, 172.
Tropp, Martin, 318.
Tuck, Donald H., 38, 39, 204, 205.
Turner, David G., 305.
Tweney, George H., 279.
Tyler, J.E.A., 339.

Urang, Gunnar, 206.

Van Vogt, A.E., 341.
Viggiano, Michael, 6.
Visiak, E.H., 276.

Wagar, W. Warren, 362.
Walker, Dale L., 277, 278.
Walling, William A., 319.
Walsh, Chad, 118.
Warner, Harry, Jr., 173.
Warner, Sylvia Townsend, 367.
Watkins, A.H., 363.
Watney, John, 311.
Watt, Donald, 270.
Weinberg, Robert E., 53, 71, 119, 185, 246, 267.
Wells, Geoffrey H., 364.
Wentz, Walter J., 301.
Wertham, Fredric, 182.
West Richard C., 340.
Wetzel, George, 295.
Whyte, Andrew Adams, 40.
Williams, Raymond, 308.
Williams, Sidney, 341.

TITLE INDEX

This short-title index includes all book titles cited in the main entries. Numbers refer to entry code number.